"I think this should be
to improve their negotia
negotiating in daily life.'

MW00774962

Chairman and CEO (retired), Schnuck Markets

"A lively and insightful guide to a skill all negotiators need to
acquire: negotiation in the service of their clients."
—R. H. Helmholz,
Professor at Law in the University of Chicago

"Read and reread this book! Cash is a master of the game. The
insights and distinctions are priceless!"
—Keith J Cunningham,
Best Selling Author of *The Road Less Stupid*

"After 40 years of lawyering and teaching, and almost
1000 mediations, I thought I had read it all, heard it all, seen
it all. I couldn't believe how much I learned from this book."
—Karen Tokarz,
Washington University School of Law

"*Negotiation as a Martial Art* likens a negotiation to a zen-like
understanding between two or more people. Social psycho-
logy in action."
—James W Pennebaker,
Regents Centennial Professor,
University of Texas at Austin

NEGOTIATION

— AS A —

Martial Art

TECHNIQUES TO MASTER THE
ART OF HUMAN EXCHANGE

CASH NICKERSON

**MADE FOR
SUCCESS**

Made for Success Publishing
P.O. Box 1775 Issaquah, WA 98027
www.MadeForSuccessPublishing.com

Distributed by Made for Success Publishing

First Printing

Library of Congress Cataloging-in-Publication data
Nickerson, Cash
  NEGOTIATION AS A MARTAIL ART: Techniques to Master
  the Art of Human Exchange
  p. cm.

  LCCN: 2021938179
  ISBN: 978-1-64146-626-4 (*Paperback*)
  ISBN: 978-1-64146-668-4 (*eBook*)
  ISBN: 978-1-64146-669-1 (*Audiobook*)

Printed in the United States of America

For further information contact Made for Success Publishing
+14255266480 or email service@madeforsuccess.net

Table of Contents

AUTHOR'S NOTE

YOU CAN'T WRITE about negotiation without considering your position *vis-a-vis* the seminal book, *Getting to Yes: Negotiating Agreement Without Giving In* by Roger Fisher and William Ury.[1] Written over 30 years ago, this book taught us several valuable lessons: Separate the people from the problem, focus on interests and not positions, invent multiple options in looking for mutual gain, and insist on objective standards. The book also formally introduced the concept of BATNA, an acronym for "best alternative to a negotiated agreement." *Getting to Yes* sought to change negotiations from an adversarial tug of war to cooperative problem-solving. It is a great book as a foundation for negotiating theory and practice. It has several limitations, however, including the phrase "separate the people from the problem." For me, and in my experience, the people often *are* the problem, and you have to deal with both the people and the problem.

Therefore, in *Negotiation as a Martial Art*, I focus on the people as the issue and explore the opportunities that people tactics and soft skills have to improve your position. Once you separate the people from the problem, what do you do? *Getting to Yes* says you can be hard on the problem and soft on the people. That is overly simplistic to those of us who negotiate for a living, as I have. In this book, I will introduce a matrix of hard and soft approaches when it comes to negotiations. In this book, I will discuss several key concepts, including structured people tactics, inventing, excelling at multiple options, and developing a better understanding of what we and what they want.

This book also places a lot of focus on the pre-negotiation stage. It explores the importance of the "why." Understanding "why" others want something or you want something is critical. Suppose you want to buy a car. Why do you need it? Do you need it to commute to work? Do you need it to drive around on a Saturday night? Do you need it for your job? Which of those motivations is most important? A good salesperson will explore these issues to help find a fit for you. Your motivations for buying a car come into play in your selection and become part of the negotiation. If your motive is to commute, the city gas mileage will be important. If the salesperson pushes a car for Saturday night, when you understand your motivations and their priority, you will have confidence negotiating stronger on price for the Saturday night car because ongoing expense is an issue.

The "why" is part of the backstory in negotiations. This book describes techniques to find the backstories that are so important in negotiations. There are always backstories. And to get at these, I reiterate the critical usage of the tool of listening. You can truly empower yourself with listening.

I have seen a topic that has surfaced in negotiation literature called Investigative Negotiation. In negotiation literature, this topic is described as a tactic. Negotiation experts say, "Here is something you can try under these circumstances." I don't see it that way at all. For me, the approach I describe is not a tactic; it is a way of life that carries over into negotiation. These principles will help you not only become a better negotiator but will assist you to become a better person. Negotiation is a socially rich experience woven into our everyday life.

This book is based on 36 years of experience as a businessperson, entrepreneur, lawyer, and professor. I have taught negotiation skills to lawyers as a Professor of Practice at Washington University School of Law for four years. The book is not primarily conceptual. It is designed to help you change your behavior and learn to practice differently so you will attain more positive successes. Someone read one of my listening books and said it was repetitive and obvious. Fair enough. That is true. But that is because the purpose of the book is not about reading to understand concepts but to take action by doing. In this book, I provide some specific questions and tactics that you can adopt that will make you negotiate better.

I guarantee it.

INTRODUCTION

Knowledge speaks. Wisdom listens.
—Jimi Hendrix

THE SIMPLE TRUTH is that often we don't really know what we want, but we think we know. And because we don't know what we want, but we think we know, we interact with others in deals and disputes chasing blurred objectives. But the process of negotiation, when properly pursued, can be a process of joint self-discovery by both parties, one that leads us closer to what we want and also brings to our counterparty or parties what they want.

The path of that process begins with the recognition of this fact: that we don't know what we want. This recognition is followed by a period of intellectual curiosity during which we ask and listen, culminating in the final stage of preparation, reflection, and classic problem-solving techniques. The success of this process is dependent on shifting our thinking from *"what we want"* to *"why we want it"* and then back again to *"what we want."* This dynamic process is one of investigation and discovery. It involves not just introspection but also an examination of the counterparty's interests and motivations.

Understanding the "why" requires a lot of preparation. This preparation comes in the form of examining the underlying motivations you have and also, the underlying motivations of your counterparty. You need to develop the mentality of an investigative journalist. With this perspective, you become proficient at asking questions of others and even of yourself. You need to become proficient at listening to others and to yourself. By engaging in this type of negotiation strategy and style, you can create and promote a healthy climate of intellectual curiosity and openness throughout the negotiation process. Negotiation needs to be viewed as a process of discovery.

Case Study #1: The Two-Year-Old and the Red Car

A two-year-old toddler is going to have breakfast with her two cousins—both also two years old—and her father. Knowing the importance of keeping young children occupied, Dad brings three kid-pleasing toys: a small red car, a fluffy stuffed monkey, and a toy cell phone.

Since they all are his daughter's toys, her father gives her the first choice of which toy she wants to have. She doesn't hesitate as she picks the fluffy stuffed monkey. One of the cousins picks the red car while the other cousin picks the toy cell phone. All is fine—briefly. Each toddler got what they wanted and was happy with their choice. And then things started to fall apart.

The cousin who picked the red car enjoyed it greatly and made loud "vroom" noises as she rolled it back and forth across the breakfast table. The two-year-old daughter, seeing the obvious happiness of her cousin as she played with the red car, tossed her fluffy stuffed monkey on the floor and burst into tears, demanding the red car instead.

But she had the first pick; how could she now be upset? She had chosen the fluffy stuffed monkey. She was happy with her selection. She got what she wanted. She got the toy she chose. So, what happened?

What happened was this: What the two-year-old really wanted was to have the most fun. As soon as she saw that a different toy gave someone else more fun than she was having, she wanted that toy. Perhaps, given they were her toys, what she wanted was complete control over all the toys. She wanted the power. Why did she want the fluffy stuffed monkey? She wanted control over the situation. I am willing to bet that if you asked the two-year-old why she wanted the fluffy stuffed monkey, she would simply have said, "Because it is mine."

"Well, that is typical for a child," you may say.

Not necessarily. Over a 36-year career, I have seen this similar human behavior in many negotiations by seasoned business executives. The observed behavior is an outward expression of desire that is not consistent with true intentions. The child appears to have made a choice based upon what she wanted. But really, the child wanted control of the outcome because these were her toys. The world of business is very similar. Often what appears to be about choice is about control over choices.

Case Study #2: It's Not Always About the Numbers

As a young lawyer, I witnessed a remarkable negotiation in which a 60-plus-year-old, highly educated, seasoned, and experienced senior executive (I'll call him "the maven") of a mega-corporation grossly overspent on an acquisition. That was my first true glimpse into the critical importance of understanding the "why" before drawing conclusions about the "what."

The maven opened the acquisition process with a bid of several hundred million dollars for a company that had been started by an entrepreneur and had grown successfully over the years, until it was now a large and significant business that became a publicly-traded company. The financial analysis of that business showed it could be worth another 50% more over the initial acquisition bid, which was slightly at a premium to its public stock price.

In response to the offer from the maven, the entrepreneur owner said, "Sorry, my company is not for sale."

The maven from the much larger company raised the bid 50% higher but still in line with the financial analysis. The entrepreneur again responded the same way, saying, "Sorry, my company is not for sale."

The maven then asked, "How much do you want?"

The entrepreneur said at a later time that the figure he should ask for his company had come to him in a dream. In the present negotiation, he followed that dream and asked for three times the original bid, adding that it was his final number, take it or leave it.

Now the ball was squarely in the maven's court. He had a choice. Since the deal no longer made financial sense, he could walk away from the acquisition. But that's not what happened. The maven took the deal back to his financial team and explained away the financial discrepancy, reframing the acquisition as a "strategic deal." He even redid the assumptions of the financial analysis, which created new industry distinctions to reach the result he wanted. The acquisition of the company was made. Of course, the deal was ultimately a disaster and divested at a substantial loss.

So, what happened? Why did a man who was an experienced and successful senior executive make such a disastrous acquisition, risking far more of his own company's financial resources than the numbers warranted? The answer again lies in the "why" before the "what" principle of negotiation.

Beware the Strategic Deal

As a young lawyer with a strong business sense and an MBA, after graduating and entering the business world, I thought, "Wow, the real world sure is different than business school!"

So, I set out to understand why. Why did poor business decisions happen? Why did some deals go so badly wrong? Why did some seemingly rational, experienced leaders and decision-makers make such disastrous acquisitions? I have said for years in speeches and to business classes to "beware the strategic deal." If someone says a deal is "strategic" so you don't need to be concerned about the numbers, your antenna should quiver.

Back to our maven and why he overpaid for his acquisition. Why did he go against the numbers generated by his own financial team? Why did this deal happen? At the end of the day, after asking lots of questions, an answer emerged. There was a new CEO coming into the maven's company. There was lots of cash on the balance sheet. I came to believe that the maven, who had been passed over for the CEO job, was determined to design the future of the company and spend the treasury before the new CEO came. And so he did.

What did our maven really want? He wanted control over the future strategy of his huge company. Just like the two-year-old wanting control over the happiness of her cousins because the toys were all hers, the maven wanted to control the future of the company by making financial decisions because he still could.

When a Deal Seems to Make No Financial Sense

I got to know the entrepreneur involved and spent time after the deal trying to understand what he thought and what he wanted, as well as what he thought the maven wanted. The first thing he admitted was that even though an asking price for his company had come to him in a dream, he had actually made the number up that he presented to the maven—he pulled it out of a hat.

Why? Because he had figured out that the deal he was negotiating had nothing to do with numbers. What he discerned from the maven and the maven's interactions with him was that this deal was going to happen, no matter what numbers were on the table. The maven wanted control over the future of the company, so the entrepreneur could probably get whatever terms he wanted for his company. He discerned this in part because no matter what he said, the maven had a comeback. The maven was sword-drawn and aggressive the entire time. I only remember the maven asking one question. When all else had failed, he said, "How much do you want?" Had the maven started with this question, the outcome would have been very different. But the maven's aggressive "I must have this" approach was obvious to the entrepreneur, who, as a kid, learned to trade on a playground and not in a classroom.

The Power of Asking "Why"

The entrepreneur had a high school education. But as simple as his formal education appeared, he was very good at asking why. And I remember him asking a lot of "whys" in the negotiations with the maven. He was distrustful, as he explained to me, of these highly educated folks coming down to his company to buy it. That distrust translated into skepticism which the business maven interpreted as solvable by just increasing the price. The entrepreneur asked, "Why my company?" "Why is my company worthy of your attention?" "Why is it worth so much?" "Why are you interested in my industry?" "Why me and not one of my competitors?"

The entrepreneur listened very carefully to the answers the maven gave him to those questions and concluded the maven had to have this deal. So, even with his multiple graduate degrees from the best schools in America, the maven "lost" and the entrepreneur with no formal education "won." His success was due to powerful listening skills combined with asking the "why" questions first.

Discover the "Why" First

The "as is" or current state when it comes to negotiation is inefficient, and outcomes are hard to define as successful or not successful without an analysis. One of the assignments I give my class is to define "success" in a negotiation. I ask for it at the beginning of class and then have them refine it as the class continues right up until the very end. When is the last time you wrote down what success would be in a negotiation before you engage in the process? Defining success will help you get at the "why" as well as the "what" because the reality is that we often don't know what we want. As a result, we frequently employ others, either formally or informally, to help us get what we think we want. We send advocates in the form of accountants, lawyers, spouses, and friends to help us get these things we think we want. These intermediaries play an important role in asking "why" questions in the discovery process.

However, while our third parties are out chasing what we think we want, they are engaging with third parties who are pursuing what their principals think they want. In other words, when you only focus on wants, underlying motivations are not uncovered, and therefore everyone guesses why someone wants what they want, or they just demand what is wanted. One spouse asks the other who is going to the grocery store to pick up some tomatoes. The spouse cruises through the store and spies a can of tomatoes on the shelf and throws them in the cart. The shopping spouse returns with the groceries, and as they unpack them together, the non-shopping spouse says, "Where are the tomatoes?" The shopping spouse holds up the can. The spouse who needed the tomatoes that night says, "How am I going to put those in a salad?"

Reflect on that simple example and you begin to understand why we spend so much money on third parties to help us with transactions, dispute resolution, and deal consummation and why we or others on our teams are so dissatisfied with what we get. Often what ultimately happens is not what we intended. We never understood the "why" and so got a suboptimal "what."

Adding asking and listening to the mix. The approach to understanding the significance of "why" to "what" is an iterative process. It is fundamentally a process that involves a lot of asking. And any process associated with asking invokes listening. I have written two books about listening, *Listening as a Martial Art*[1] and *The Samurai Listener*[2]. This current book, *Negotiation as a Martial Art,* will expand further on the critical component of listening—listening to yourself, to others on your team, to your advisors, to your counterparties, to their teammates, and their advisors. Listening in these contexts as described in my *Listening* books is not about hearing, but about sensing meanings, feelings, and intentions behind words. It is the art of listening in its broadest sense that helps you get to the "why."

From rational to "what are they thinking?" If you reflect on either your own negotiations, negotiations where you have been an intermediary, or negotiations you have watched on media, ask yourself if most rational actors sit down with rational positions and clear underlying interests. Or do you find yourself more often scratching your head asking, "What are they thinking; what is going on?"

Look for Plato's "Backstory" or "Other" World

In my over 36 years of experience, I have come to know that in negotiations there is often a backstory. Like Plato's cave analogy, there is frequently a world we see and a world we don't see, but this other world is really driving what is going on in many negotiations. In discussing enlightenment, Plato described the world that everyone sees as not being the real world. The world everyone sees, he explains, is the wall of a cave that has light from a fire reflecting on it. Between the fire and the people who are facing the wall are various objects. So, people facing the wall see shadows that are not the things themselves. Enlightened people (freed from just sitting and staring at the cave wall) see the objects themselves. When someone tells you what they want but not why, you may well be looking at a shadow and thinking it is real. But there is a real object behind you: literally, it is a backstory.

If you don't know what that backstory is, or if you don't uncover its hidden elements, then you are going to be frustrated as you work through proposals and counterproposals. Backstories can be hard to discern, but through asking "why" and using advanced listening skills, you can discover in which deals they exist. You may even be able to uncover and reveal the backstory itself.

There is also another key element at play here. And that is our own backstory. Asking ourselves "why" can lead to important self-discovery. We often don't know or realize what WE want, like the young child who thinks she wants the fluffy stuffed monkey. Pushing ourselves to examine what we want and, most importantly, why we want it—what our underlying motivation is—helps uncover our own desires, which in turn helps us with what to prioritize and insist upon and what to trade.

What to Consider—Interests or Positions?

Consider this well-known example in politics of the clash between interests and positions. President Trump promised a wall on the border but needed the Democrats to get it done. The Democrats pushed back, questioning its efficacy, cost, and effectiveness, and so refused to support it. Republicans tried to point to previous Democratic support for a border "fence" and it was "game on." Modern negotiation strategies based on books like *Getting to Yes*[3] say to consider interests and not positions. "No problem!" you say. The underlying interest involves national border security. Great, so the rational solution lies in exploring various methods of improving border security.

There are several related issues in providing for border security, such as how drugs come into the country and how the undocumented enter. A border wall may be a part of the solution, but rationally speaking, there are a lot of breakthrough ideas that are more effective and can now come forward as solutions and resolve the impasse. So, those ideas should be brought forward.

Simple, right? Textbook negotiation solution. Except none of that happens. Why not?

There is clearly a backstory at work. Positions and interests are not as they appear. Some might say that President Trump had no interest in negotiating, but he would say the same about the Democrats. Trump's "why" had to do with fulfilling a campaign promise and securing the support of his base in states like Arizona and Texas, as well as sowing fear. Was the "why" for the Democrats based on a completely different view of a path forward for immigrants and immigration, or was it fueled by election promises and opposition to Trump's goals? There could have been points of agreement in the range between these two positions. But was it about positions or interests? In the end, it was about the people and their interests. There was no separating the people from the problem. The people *were* the problem. Of course, Biden was elected later and in one of his first acts, he lifted Trump's border policies and halted the wall. This proves the point that people's interests take precedence. Soon a border crisis ensued. The people pursuing their interests were the problem.

In all the situations I describe in the book, one truth will emerge. A better understanding of what you want—and, if you are an intermediary, a better understanding of what your principal wants—will put you in a stronger position to deal with negotiation scenarios. The backstories of parties and counterparties can surface as you engage in "why" analysis and guide strategies toward successful outcomes.

Master Asking "Why" and Listening to the Answers

I have been doing deals for over three decades as a lawyer, entrepreneur, business executive, in-house attorney, principal, and deal broker. These deals have not just been transactions; they have also included litigation settlements, alternative dispute negotiations, and mediations. I have been involved in more transactions than I can remember. I have "won" and I have "lost." But more than anything else, I have learned.

I have studied the deals and the soft skill of negotiation and associated communications. I have read numerous books on negotiations, and I have attended many seminars. I have lectured and taught negotiations to business teams and law students. I have spent four years, while still doing deals, teaching a class called "Domestic and International Business Lawyering, Listening, Writing and Negotiating." I have learned a lot from teaching that class to some of the brightest law students in the country.

The key principles I have learned in these years of doing, practicing, studying, and teaching are in this book. Based on all those years, there is no question in my mind that you can dramatically improve your negotiations and gain more successful outcomes by mastering asking "why" and listening to the answers. Focusing on "why" first and then moving to "what" uncovers the backstories of both parties and leads to goal clarification.

Why Negotiation as a Martial Art?

My neighborhood in Pittsburgh was interesting. I remember we had one really big kid named Sid (I dedicated this book to what he forced me to learn). In any confrontation, he would just get on top of you, and you couldn't move him. Sid was huge and heavy.

Years later, I remember vividly the first time in martial arts when I tried to move someone huge and heavy who was on top of me, just like back when I was trying to move Sid. And then I learned one of my most important lessons. I will never forget the day I learned how to stop trying to move the big guy off of me and instead learned to move myself. It was like a lightning bolt in my head. I tell the story in Chapter 2.

How often do we push against an immovable wall because we think we want something, but we really haven't thought through our own motivations or those of our opponent? What I wanted was Sid off of me. Why was I trying to move Sid? Because he was heavy, and it hurt. To remove that "Sid" pain was to want to get out from under him. Sid was counting on my opposition to him. He was expecting my pushback. He wanted me to try to move him off me so I could get free. But nobody could move Sid.

Here's the revelation. I didn't have to move Sid. I could move MYSELF! Unfortunately for my childhood, I didn't learn that lesson until much later in life.

Learning to get in touch with yourself and your position allows you to wiggle your way out. Where are they, where are you? What can you move? You feel yourself and you feel them, and you wiggle using tactics in this book. Suddenly, the weight is gone, the pain is gone, and you are free; not because you moved Sid but because you moved what you could move. You moved yourself. You changed your position, and you got what you really wanted.

And that's what *Negotiation as a Martial Art* is all about—shifting the landscape, questioning the motivations, uncovering the backstory, and ultimately engaging in a new paradigm. You engage in negotiation by understanding the people aspects and the soft skills. Negotiation becomes a martial art driven by discovery and fluidity, true qualities of the martial arts.

CHAPTER 1

BE LIKE WATER

In the struggle between the stone and water, in time, the water wins.

—Japanese Proverb

Silence Yourself

As a lifetime practicing martial artist, I find myself constantly using lessons from various martial arts to help me in the world of work. One of the most common themes running through all martial arts from American Kenpo and Karate to Judo, Brazilian Jiu Jitsu, Kickboxing, and Systema is the silencing of your "self."

Martial arts are fundamentally defensive. They arose in cultures during those times when oppressed populations were forbidden weapons. Hence, the famed bare fists of Karate—which literally means "empty hand." To be able to defend yourself, you need to be relaxed. No stress. You need to be empty. You need to be silent. In that way, you can feel and sense others more acutely. You can be prepared for anything without being blocked by your own thoughts and senses. In a physical confrontation, if you are tense or distracted by the planning and anticipation of your next move toward your opponent, you are much more likely to be hit.

To achieve that state of empty quiet, martial artists meditate. They learn to breathe. They learn to be open. They learn to be, as Bruce Lee said, "like water." When you are like water you take whatever shape you need to become. You become like water to win. As the quote at the beginning of this chapter notes, it is the stone that gets shaped by the water. The water is fine.

Great martial artists and great negotiators don't give away their position or strategy. As an example, it is not unusual for a martial artist to be better at some things than others because different styles have different advantages and disadvantages. Jiu Jitsu practitioners are great on the ground and good at grappling. Karate is a stand-up art with little focus on the ground. Great competitors will not show their strength because it also may display a weakness. If they posture like a wrestler, they have shown they prefer the ground. If they posture like a boxer, they expose themselves as someone who prefers standing and should be taken to the ground. Displaying your strength can expose your vulnerability.

How to be like water? Relax without showing strength or weakness.

I recall attending a play in New York City Times Square with my business partner at the time, accompanied by his girlfriend and my wife. It was a limited production play of *Glengarry Glen Ross* with Liev Schreiber and Alan Alda in leading roles. After the fantastic show, the audience exited into Times Square around midnight. I was about 10 feet away from my wife and my business partner's girlfriend when I observed a man studying them. He seemed to be looking at their purses and seeing who was around them. I could sense he was about to make a move, so I immediately closed the gap and stood between him and the women. I looked him in the eye and smiled and put out my hand to shake his hand, and I said, "Hey, how you doing?" He put out his hand and shook mine, and I just said, "There is nothing for you here." He shook my hand for a little longer than you would expect, and then smiled and walked away. This is a perfect example of the power of a "be like water" strategy. I wasn't threatening. I wasn't afraid, but he could tell from my gentle handshake that I knew and felt his intentions. I think he sensed only someone with martial arts training would have no fear of him.

The Drawbacks of a "Sword Drawn" Strategy

Negotiating and selling have many commonalities. In both situations, you are trying to win someone over to your position. You are trying to get them to agree to something they have not agreed to yet. You are trying to change the behavior of your counterparty.

Suppose you are on a sales call and meeting with a prospect. Imagine you open with, "I want to sell you this and that, and here's why it's right for you, and here's why you should buy it right now."

Here's what you are doing. You are doing all the talking. You are pushing, you are controlling, you are being a rock and a hard stone. By approaching your prospect this way, you are coming with "sword drawn." What does that mean? How is this perceived by your counterparty? This approach is aggressive, could even be perceived as combative, and it will likely elicit the opposite reaction from the one you were hoping to achieve.

People try to sell and convince me with "sword drawn" every day. They not only do it in person but also via email, voice messages, phone calls, lots of different communication methods. When you approach negotiation as a combative sale, you will likely get pushback and strong defensiveness in your counterparty. Whether this happens in sales or whether it happens in negotiations, it can be the beginning of the end of a mutually beneficial outcome.

A Defensive Response

What happens if you are on the other side of that conversation? What happens if you are the buyer? What happens when you are the party targeted for convincing? When someone tries to convince you or sell you offensively, what do you do? Simple. You defend yourself. You raise your shield. You become immediately skeptical. You think of reasons not to buy and not to believe.

When I am the buyer, the party you are trying to convince, I react to your approach with a strong defensive counter of my own. We may even enter fighting mode. The sale and purchase opportunities disappear. The opportunity to convince and persuade disappears, replaced by a dominating posture that often pushes the parties' positions apart.

Broken Negotiations

In negotiation, the counterparty reacts to the "sword drawn" with a "raised shield," and the result is often a broken negotiation. There is no build-up of trust; therefore, it's not likely to reach a valuable outcome.

This strategy is even more counterproductive when you are trying to sell something or, more importantly, negotiate to replace an existing product or service. Remember, the buyer has already made the purchase once. The counterparty has already completed what they considered to be a successful negotiation once. By coming in "sword drawn," you are now also sending a message that the original purchase or the original deal was somehow the result of the buyer's or counterparty's initial bad decision. You are challenging the buyer. You are challenging the person sitting across from you at the negotiating table, attacking their judgment and ego. At least, that is how it will be perceived.

Now consider a different strategy.

The Ask and Listen Strategy: Finding Openings Like Water Finding Holes

Imagine you enter your negotiation with questions. You come in like water. You are prepared but not presuming your outcome by making demands of what you want. Suppose, instead, you ask good questions. What are good questions? Those that find an opening.

Finding openings can be the hardest part of a negotiation, and asking and listening offer the best opening. If you are specific about exactly what you want at the outset, you may leave something important remaining on the table. If you ask for too much, the negotiation may end quickly.

One of the most common tactics is to try to get the other side to speak first. The problem is that everyone tries this. I teach negotiation as a Professor of Practice at a highly ranked law school. I can tell that my students have already heard this strategy many times before: "Whatever you do, don't give the first number." How often have you heard the phrase, "Whoever speaks first loses." I know you have also heard the phrase, "The higher you start, the better deal you get," or "Anchor high."

You see this in martial arts contests like in the Ultimate Fighting Championship (UFC) or in bad boxing or wrestling matches. The fighters just circle each other, waiting for the other side to do something. The audience boos because nothing happens. There is no action. There is no resolution.

To open well, it is important to get the other side talking. But what I found as a consequence was that the negotiation teams in my class were often afraid to talk about anything substantive and got bogged down in what they perceived as safe peripheral matters. They clung to small matters out of fear of being the first to say what they wanted. So, they would talk about anything but the substance of what they wanted. Artful asking and listening can provide that opening if you ask the right questions. Good questions are those that reveal some state of dissatisfaction in the other party that leads to an opening for you.

When you open in this manner, you are letting the other party in the negotiation lead. But you need to let them lead in a way that doesn't appear you are trying to corner them. This means asking open-ended questions, not closed-ended ones. Think of closed-ended questions as those that can be answered yes or no, while open-ended questions welcome narrative.

If you imagine a trial, think of open-ended questions like those you are allowed to ask of your own witness and the closed-ended questions as cross-examination type of questions. Here are some business examples:

Open-ended question: "Why are you interested in buying ABC enterprises?"

Closed-ended question: "You are just buying this company so you can sell off its divisions, right?"

People are more receptive to open-ended questions, although there is a time to use each of these types. Asking questions, especially open-ended ones, draws out your counterparty. It creates an atmosphere where your counterparty thinks and believes that the ideas are theirs. And, they also have already bought into these ideas. When you push your own ideas, you make the other party defensive. Selling, and by extension negotiating, are in the nature of martial arts. In martial arts, the search for that opening in your opponent is a patient one that eventually yields results for both parties.

In this search for openings, we can borrow from classic sales techniques, such as using questions to uncover common interests and other methods for establishing trust. If you have researched your counterparty, you will be able to make "six degrees of separation connections" to develop trust. You might say, "I see you are connected with Courtney from Adams and Smith; she is a good friend of mine. How do you know her?" This early small talk is part of the dance that most people like and feel comfortable with.

"I see you went to UVA; did you know Bob? He was there around when you were."

"I know you worked on the Texaco deal. Did you work with Alice Jones?"

"I saw that you are a pilot. What is your favorite plane?"

Negotiation is a human process, and thus rich in human interaction. Showing your human side, establishing that you care, and demonstrating empathy all make the human being across from you more comfortable.

Negotiations are personal and emotional, no matter how much money is involved. Work to elicit that human side of negotiations early so you can begin to build trust. In the book *Whale Done*, Ken Blanchard says the key to training killer whales is within the very first step, you must convince the whale you mean them no harm.[1] Humans are a lot like killer whales. It's important that they do not feel threatened. Truth be told, I am a firm believer in breaking tension with humor as well, which creates a relaxed environment in which people feel safe.

Some openings I have used are: "So, why are we here?"

I have diffused tension with a simple, "So what is up?" Or a simple, "How can I (or we) help?"

Starting with a "concierge" negotiation tone will more likely get them working with you. Entering with demands puts everyone in their corner.

Openings to negotiations should be simple, non-threatening, inviting, and used to establish trust.

The Art of Becoming Empty

If and when you find the right opening—and this takes practice—you have to become empty and listen. You have to be so empty that you won't even have to take a single note. You will concentrate so hard on listening that you will not only listen, but you will remember everything you heard. Then, and only then, will you connect your services, your products, and your perspective with the other person's desires and wants. You need to get them talking.

If you have engaged in this "ask and listen" strategy, you will find and clearly see openings. Openings are opportunities or conceptual gaps where you can test and interject and try to match their needs and desires with yours. Once you find an opening, you may well use a more closed-ended question that elicits a yes or no answer.

Using the art of becoming empty to find the best opening is a key reason you need to be so intensely prepared with the features and benefits of your product or service. You must be clear on your negotiating position. You need to be so well prepared that introducing these as needs and opportunities will be effortless. It will be natural. You will be leading, but the other party will believe that the lead is theirs. When you behave and act this way, the other party will feel like they are teaching you. And you will begin to feel like the student in the relationship. This is greatness.

Takeaway

Openings require open-ended questions and a bit of small talk. Don't come into a sales call or negotiation with your sword drawn. Come in empty-handed. Come in formless and shapeless, like water. Come in prepared to ask evoking questions that will lead to the discovery of information you can use to your advantage. Uncover the other party's true desires and dissatisfactions, and you will find what they really want. You will uncover all of the important backstories.

Come in ready to listen with complete openness until the opportunity to present your product, service, or position arises. At all times, if you listen hard enough, you will remember everything. Don't rush. Don't jump the gun. Be patient.

Be like water.

CHAPTER 2

ADJUSTING YOUR OWN POSITION

*…rock bottom became a solid foundation
on which I rebuilt my life.*

—J.K. Rowling

Negotiating Leverage Born From Martial Arts Defense

It was a crisp morning in August in the Algonquin Forest about three hours north of Toronto. The smell of mud and grass hung in the chilly air as we grappled with each other. This martial arts camp was a bi-annual event that drew martial arts enthusiasts from across the globe.

It was a program of intense martial arts training. We all trained in these martial arts for self-defense in the woods, in the lake, in daylight, at dusk, and in the deep dark of forest nights.

One chilly morning, we were practicing groundwork—training that looked very much like wrestling to those who didn't study martial arts.

One-on-One

Some of us had trained in Brazilian Jiu Jitsu, and others had wrestling backgrounds. We trained one-on-one in pairs in which we attacked and defended. We did this groundwork without standing up, just breathing and moving. The goal was clear—avoid submission or getting pinned down. In this exercise, I discovered the key to unlocking deadlock. As interesting and challenging as one-on-one work was, we were next put in a particular position that taught me an important lesson, one that I have used to help me in negotiating. I am confident it can be an important key that can unlock negotiating deadlocks. In learning this lesson, I finally solved the Sid problem from my youth.

Shifting an "Impossible" Weight

One person lay on the ground, in whatever position they chose. Some chose to lie on their back, some on their side, and some on their stomach. Next, others in the group got on top of the person on the ground, one by one. First, there were two on top. Then there were three. Then it became four. Then as many as six people would pile on top of that person lying on the ground. The people on top didn't move. They just lay on top with all their weight pressing down passively. The ultimate challenge was to escape from under that seemingly impossible weight.

When a ground fighting match was one-on-one, if you were bigger than the other party on top, you could move them around. If your technique was superior, you could dominate them. But when there were six people on top of you, there was one thing you couldn't do. You couldn't move them. This is the point of the exercise. If you tried to move them, you would be suffocated as you ran out of energy to breathe. You can't move the weight on top of you. You can't move the unmovable people. So when you have the weight of six people on you, what is the only thing you can do?

When Faced With the Immovable—
Move Yourself

You can try to find gaps so you can move yourself. How do you go about this? The first task is to figure out what part of yourself you can move. What part of you is free? Maybe you can move one of your feet. Maybe you can move one of your hands. Maybe you can only move a finger.

There is always something in your body you can move, no matter how small. There is always something you can shift, even slightly, into a better position. Movement, any movement, is critical to preserving your energy, relieving your breathing, and angling for a position from which you can begin to extricate yourself. You have to move so you can survive.

The only wrong move in this challenge is to try to lift off the pile of bodies pressing down on you. The only wrong move is to focus on the pile. You can't move the pile. You have to move yourself. You need to wiggle. Wiggling is defined by *Webster's Dictionary* as "1: to move to and fro with quick jerky or shaking motions: jiggle. 2: to proceed with or as if with twisting and turning movements."[1] When you wiggle, and great Jiu Jitsu practitioners are masterful wigglers, you move what you can as fast and disruptively as you are able until something breaks free.

The process is one of segmentation. The wall of bodies has pieces and parts. Since you are under the wall, you need to be attentive to where there is pressure and where there is not. What do you feel? Where is the pain? How can you move to relieve the pain? Where do you feel gaps? Where is there light? If you feel pain in a joint, it is because the joint is not meant to move in that direction. Can you twist your arm little by little so the tension on it is aligned with how the joint is meant to move? Start with the worst pain and work from those as priorities. With Sid or any other large person, you move yourself against the ground little by little, eliminating pain points as you move and work to slide and wiggle yourself out from the bottom of the weight, out from being underneath Sid. You use Sid's weight to help you with that wiggling and sliding campaign. Eventually, his weight pulls him to the ground as you wiggle out from under him.

From the Martial Arts Arena
to the Negotiating Table

In negotiations, we need to remind ourselves that trying to move the other party, like trying to move the stack of six people, is the worst thing to do. As you attempt to push others to improve your position, what happens? The opposition becomes heavier. You become more tired with every push. The best negotiation option for you is to examine your own position and look for any small wins you can find. This is "wiggle-room" time. Ask yourself:

What can you change?

What can you give up to get to a better position?

What negotiating gap can you find?

This is not your time to relax, not time to be calm water, but to be frothy water. You have to be nimble. You need to ask rapid-fire, closed-end questions to open a door that is hard to open. You discombobulate without offending because you are offering ways to move yourself. You brainstorm ways to get something open with them, while recognizing your inferior position. What you are looking to find are variables that you don't know about. The rapid-fire questions help you find opportunities. You are creating space by creating possibilities because you are getting deeper and deeper behind interests and positions and getting to know the people you are negotiating with better and better. This spontaneous brainstorming should lead you to find interests, sub-interests, and what is behind some impediments. Underlying feelings and motivations need to be unearthed and discovered. In this way, negotiation is a discovery process.

When Your Opponent is More Powerful

This approach is especially important in situations where the other side is much more powerful than you are. For example, I own several high-rise condominiums. As a result of my ownership position, I have served on four boards that govern these condominiums in multiple cities and even in different countries. One of the most common challenges for the owners of condominiums is the threat of development on an adjacent property. Development can and often does bring with it negatives for condominium owners— everything from increased population density to blocked views, reduced sunlight, additional traffic, noise, and countless other issues.

Unfortunately, all too often the developers tend to hold all the cards. This is even more likely if the developer isn't seeking a zoning change. Condominium owners are in a weaker position than the developers. What happens? Condominium owners dig in their heels, and through their associations they attempt to "just say no" to any proposed development. However, if the building is in a central business district or if the developer has an existing relationship with the city, the "no" of the condo owners is going to fall on deaf ears and that adjacent property will be developed.

All too often this "just say no" strategy is doomed to fail. I have watched associations that use this strategy lose any say in what happens next door to their condominiums. At the end of the fight, like the person at the bottom of the human pile who tries to push the six people off of them, the condo board and the owners end up frustrated, tired, and angry.

The "Wiggle Contingency" Strategy

The enlightened approach to such negotiations is to recognize that you are not going to win a head-to-head battle with the developer. So you need to ask yourself, what things can you move? Where can you "wiggle"? What small part of the negotiations can you move in your favor? You can often use contingencies to find wiggle room.

A recent article published in the program on negotiation from the Harvard Law School offered an example of just such a strategy. The article was titled "Negotiation Techniques: How to Predict a Negotiator's Decisions." You can improve your negotiation skills in many ways, but knowing how you behave as a negotiator will refine your negotiation techniques." It advised that wiggle room can be created through contingencies, saying, "Be sure to create contingencies based on your opponent's potential moves. Peter Gollwitzer of New York University has shown that when people construct strategic intentions—such as, 'If she refuses to concede on price, I'll bring up the issue of delivery timing'—they more effectively and efficiently meet their goals."[2]

So, what do you include in your own wiggle strategy? Wiggling is about contingency development. Wiggling is contingency development that recognizes your head is in a vice or your opponent is King Kong. So acknowledge the mismatch. Here are some wiggle strategies.

A straightforward strategy is looking for negotiating precedents by asking the developer what kind of issues they have negotiated before. What have they given in previous negotiations?

Select one of the least important issues to them and focus only on it without other distractions. Pick your single battle—views, density, traffic, construction issues like dust, noise, light, completion timelines—and try to budge the developer on that. Get a win there. If there will be a construction site next door, then dust will accumulate. It is very hard for a developer not to agree to help with the cleaning of balconies, and it is relatively inexpensive for them to provide that help. Once you have a concession on a minor item like that, you have gotten an admission by them that they should be accountable for their impact.

After a small win, move up the ladder. Negotiate for a bigger concession from the developer. Basically, with a more powerful opponent you are pinned down, but you can wiggle your toe. They don't care about your toe. Ask for more room for your toe. Another method is to recognize the domination you face and say, "What would you tell your brother or sister to do if they were in my position?"

Takeaway

Warning: if all you do is fight the weight on top of you, you will achieve nothing. By moving yourself and seeing what you can move, you gain input and solve what you can solve. Happy Wiggles!

CHAPTER 3
FIXING YOURSELF

*I think unconscious bias is one of the
hardest things to get at.*
—Ruth Bader Ginsburg

Bias Awareness—the One Thing You Bring

The *International Journal of Conflict Management* conducted
a study to determine biases in negotiation. They found that
decision-making studies have identified ten different biases
that relate to and affect negotiation processes. Bias is a per-
vasive and difficult factor, but becoming aware of your own
biases is essential for successful negotiations. Some common
biases include physical appearance, gender, names, behaviors,
voice quality, age, sexual orientation, and religion.[1]

It's All About You

There are many uncertainties in a negotiation. It is a lot like life. You don't control quite a number of things. Most of us accept that or at least acknowledge it. So, what DO you control? Only one thing for certain: you. The one item, the one element, the one variable, the one reality, the one thing you know for sure will be in every negotiation and meeting you attend is you. You bring YOU wherever you go.

And, along with you, what do you bring? When you bring you, what else are you bringing to the party? What biases do you have? Do you even know your biases? Are you bringing trust? Are you bringing hatred? Are you bringing kindness? Are you bringing hesitation? What are you bringing? Whatever it is, it will be reacted to by others and either resisted or reproduced. This means you bring whatever your today is like; you bring your ethos, your expectations, your love or your hate—you bring your ecosystem. Bottom line is this: There is no getting around you. That means that you need to study, understand, and improve your self-awareness.

Lessons in Self-Awareness From Martial Artists

I have worked with many martial artists, and with the greatest of them I couldn't tell what they were going to do next. Even when I touched them to attempt a technique, they would somehow not provide me the response, called "support" in martial arts, that I needed. Without that support, the technique could not be performed. Great martial artists "disappear themselves."

This ability has two benefits. First, by not feeling themselves, not experiencing their internal processes, they could feel you. Second, without them feeling themselves, you could not feel them. It was as though who they were had disappeared. They were giving no clues to what their actions might be.

The same is true with a negotiation or verbal confrontation. Your anger, your tension, your feelings and how you react all serve as blocks to your ability to feel your counterparty. These same "emotional structures" provide support for your counterparty to use their technique.

Once a party finds a way to not feel themselves, they can put a structure in place or take it away at will. If you feel yourself, you won't feel your counterparty. You won't be able to feel through all of your emotional structures. To improve your ability to "disappear yourself," you need to get in touch with yourself and understand yourself better. These are the foundations for self-awareness. Here are some basics.

Shields Up!

One of the first things you are told by your parents as a child is not to talk to strangers. This is a classic introduction to a defensive posture—a "shields up" stance. Sadly, in a time of COVID-19, we are in a constant "shields up" posture. We "mask up" and socially distance as fellow humans approaching too closely could be dangerous. My daughter told me that recently she was walking outdoors on a neighborhood sidewalk with her two-year-old, and as others approached, the little girl said, "Mommy, look out, there are people coming." So this feeling of "shields up" should be readily understandable.

A similar concept is portrayed in several episodes of the classic TV series *Star Trek*. An unknown object would be picked up by the Star Trek crew and displayed on a large screen in the command center of the Starship Enterprise. Crew members would try a variety of ways to make contact with the alien object and to communicate with it. Finally, if they received no response to their attempts, Captain Kirk would order "Shields up," a defense mechanism of the starship which prevented anything from getting through which could endanger the ship and its crew.

"Shields up" for me is one of the most basic and observable body language. How often do we approach an interaction in our lives and the workplace from a "shields up" position? How often does someone have "shields up" with you?

How to recognize "Shields Up." Imagine you are speaking to someone, or perhaps to several people. As you say something, you see their faces change and their lips begin to move. You should know by this that they have stopped listening to you. You should know that they have already formulated their position and are going to respond.

But you are still talking. You may find yourself saying, "Wait, I'm not finished." They interrupt you anyway and make a response to your point. But it's not the point you were about to make. It doesn't matter. The moment you saw their faces change, they had stopped receiving information. Their shields went up. They stopped listening. Whatever you said after that event changed; it bounced off their shield.

Body language is a real key to signaling when someone is or is not receptive to you. Receptive people will appear and act interested. They have open, not crossed arms. They nod and smile. Contrast this with nonreceptive folks. They cross their arms or their legs; they are showing you a shield. They shake their heads and frown. People usually do show you how receptive they are, but you also need to be skilled at recognizing the signs.

Besides body language, people use voice intonation and word selection to demonstrate that their minds are closed on a topic. The tone of someone's voice is a key giveaway to their receptivity. People tend to raise their voices when they are not receptive. They speak in absolute and overstated terms such as "never" or "always" in opposition to your point. Their shields are up.

Emotions and Receptivity

Emotions play a key role in someone's receptivity to information. For example, you may be speaking to someone who has an emotional reaction to what you are saying. Communications with children often evoke emotional reactions. "Dad, can I go to Jack's lake house?" Shields up! You immediately become emotional because you are worried, based on what you have heard about Jack's lake house and what goes on there. You are thinking that there will be drinking by underage kids, that they will do something stupid, including driving while drinking, and someone will get hurt, potentially your son or daughter. You are not receptive, and you show it with your physical reaction and your tone of voice. Your shields are up!

In these examples, someone in the communication has ceased being receptive. They are aware, but the topic affects them in a way that closes their mind. All they see is the emotionally driven haze due to their strong feelings, such as anger. They are not receptive or open. They are not listening. Their emotions have gotten in the way. Emotions play a large part in a person's receptivity to information.

Bias Gets in the Way

Identifying bias—your own and that of others—is an important skill for negotiators.

Race, gender, sexual orientation, religion, and other biases can cause people to be nonreceptive. The same goes for you. When you encounter someone against whom you have a bias, you will not be receptive to what that individual has to say.

Everyone has someone or several people in their lives who annoy them when they talk. You want to listen, but maybe the tone of voice or the opinions of the other person bothers you. Whatever it is, when someone annoys you enough that your temper rises and you get riled up, try to start a new conversation or possibly just walk away altogether. The extremes are fairly simple to identify and recognize. What is harder to appreciate is that everyone causes some kind of reaction when they speak, as do you. Bias based on voice quality or opinions negatively impacts a person's willingness and their ability to receive information.

A Case Study in Bias from Leadership School

It was 1987, and I had just been promoted out of the law department of the Union Pacific Railroad where I had been a corporate attorney focusing on mergers and acquisitions. My new job was general manager of the air-freight division that had been acquired with the merger of the Missouri Pacific Railroad. I was in my 20s, and the employees I would be managing in the St. Louis operation were much older, in many cases twice my age, plus they all had a lot more experience.

I had spent a few years doing deals in the corporate law department, but I had not managed personnel yet. I had nearly completed my MBA, but I hadn't supervised a team or even led a major project. What do sophisticated companies do with young novices in such a situation? They send them off to leadership school! So off I went to The Center for Creative Leadership at Eckerd College in St. Petersburg, Florida. It was an outstanding experience I will never forget. And one of the many lessons it taught me was how to identify and manage bias.

One of the most instructive exercises I had at the leadership school could be called "Names withheld—code names assigned." There were 20 of us from major corporations not just in the U.S. but globally. I would like to tell you the names of all my fellow leadership learners, but I can't. Their names weren't classified or anything, but we never knew each other's names. You have to wonder as I did at the time, why the names were withheld and never disclosed.

As we came to learn, we tend to discriminate against people based on their names. When we hear a person's name, we form an immediate impression of them which is composed of everyone who shares that name you have ever met, a type of amalgam. The result is that our impression of a person when we hear their name is colored by all the people of the same name we have ever met and engaged with. This creates a bias. To eliminate the bias during leadership school, we were each assigned a Greek letter in place of a name. One of us was Omega, another Beta, a third Alpha, and so on. When you consider that something as ubiquitous as a person's name can trigger a bias, imagine all the rest of the bias hurdles we have to clear in every negotiation.

The leadership school knew that bias from our reaction to each other's names would diminish our abilities to learn and benefit from the training they provided. Although they couldn't change appearance and voice, at least one bias hurdle was removed.

A Case Study in Bias from a Family Move

Whenever people doubt me about the power and impact of names on our psyche, I like to tell them the story about my family's move from Chicago to San Francisco in the mid-1990s.

I had been offered a crisis consulting position in San Francisco for a company that was in bankruptcy in a field that I knew very well. Since my father was ill with cancer in San Diego, I wanted to be closer to him so that my children would have a chance to get to know him.

I was commuting between Chicago and the Bay Area and took a little time to look at homes. Finally, I settled upon a charming bedroom community in the East Bay and a neighborhood known as "Happy Valley." Even the elementary school was called Happy Valley. I was a little concerned about how my children would react to the move, but the minute they heard the name of their new school, they loved it.

But things didn't go according to plan. As I was bidding on the house in Happy Valley, the deal went south, and I began to focus my search on another neighborhood. When I returned home to Chicago and gave my family the update on the home search, all of my children were in tears exclaiming, "We wanted to live in Happy Valley!" None of them had ever seen Happy Valley. They knew nothing about it except its name. But they were not receptive to any other area or neighborhood. They wanted Happy Valley. They were drawn to the name, and that name affected their perception and preference dramatically.

Types of Biases

A comprehensive list of all biases is not possible in this book. But some common ones are worth mentioning and discussing. These include the following:

Physical-appearance bias. Physical appearance can create a strong bias. Study after study shows that better-looking people succeed at higher proportions than people who are not so good-looking. A better-looking lawyer has more successful results and makes more money. Taller folks win elections. There's even a reliable algorithm that determines who would be elected in a contested political race based solely on their picture from election posters. Included in the physical appearance bias are age bias, color of skin bias, gender bias, obesity bias, and hair color bias. Bias creeps into the perceptions of even the most careful and bias-conscious people.

The tone-of-voice bias. The tone of people's voices affects how and what we hear. This is why radio and TV stations hire those special "voices." This is why commercial producers hire voice experts. Tone quality matters. The more pleasing the voice tone, the more we take in from the message. The more shrill or edgy the voice, the less we are willing to absorb. The same holds true for voice volume, which must be modulated at a sufficiently loud but still pleasant level.

Behavior bias. We also have a bias against certain behaviors. We may be biased against sexual orientation. We may be biased against aggressive people or, conversely, against very shy people. This can be quite subtle. When I was at the leadership school, I learned that I was biased against introverts. How did I discover this bias in myself? A psychologist and fellow participant pointed this bias out to me. At the end of the week, we debriefed with psychologists who had observed our every move during the training. We had also been responsible for observing a peer, and that peer was in turn responsible for observing us. All this observation was designed to generate valuable feedback.

One of the peers who sat in with me during my debriefing session, I remembered well. He struck me as someone who didn't offer much help in the various exercises we were tasked with completing together. Those exercises were group activities. For example, in one exercise I was named leader. Our group was told we would be stranded on the moon and had to decide as a group what items to salvage from our damaged shuttlecraft, in order to make it to a potential rescue site. The peer in question—I never knew his name—didn't help us at all. He didn't say a word. I found his lack of participation frustrating. So what happened next was very interesting.

In my review, the psychologist said I discriminated against introverts! ME? I was the problem?

When asked, the peer said that I hadn't been as nice to him as he would have expected from the leader of the group. I responded by saying, "I'm sorry you didn't think I was nice, but we did three survival exercises and two projects together, and you said and did nothing. You did not contribute at all." He looked at me like I was crazy and said, "You never asked me what I thought."

I was stunned. I expected participants to put forth their thoughts without needing to be asked. But I had learned a valuable lesson in communication. I learned that I was biased against introverts and in favor of extroverts, people who were forthcoming with their ideas. I also learned that if you aren't communicating with an extrovert, you aren't *listening*, and if you aren't communicating with an introvert, you aren't *asking*.

Takeaway

The martial artist that doesn't experience feelings and emotions, who can "disappear themself," has actively worked over many hours with various styles or techniques of engaging. He or she knows how to "disappear" from various techniques because someone has tried that technique on them many times over the years, and they have practiced turning it into nothing. They have attained the state in which nothing about their next actions are revealed.

As a negotiator, you need to do the same thing. You need to expose yourself to lots of different people in lots of different settings. Only through these interactions will you be able to train yourself to lose your biases. Sadly, many negotiating advocates live their lives in wealthy suburbs and lack diversity awareness and training. Plan to spend time with people different than you. Ask people who are different than you how to be aware of your bias. What do they encounter that shows bias? Volunteer for activities that put you in contact with others who are different than you. Take classes on bias awareness.

There are an infinite number of factors that can make us not receptive to another person. What is important, however, is not the infinite number of biases, but the biases that are yours. Get to know your biases. Work on recognizing them. As you "disappear" your biases, your negotiations will benefit.

CHAPTER 4

PREP AND PLANNING

Don't cry because it's over. Smile because it happened.

—Dr. Seuss

Summer Camp Prep— Rediscovering the Child Within You

Successful negotiation where you address the people and the problem is more than a table, piles of reports, and weeks of research. Successful negotiation is about a different kind of preparation—the kind of prep that helps you connect with your inner self so you can find balance, stamina, innovation, and your deep creative central core to connect successfully with your workplace self. The kind of prep you can't find inside your office, but you can find it outside, at something like summer camp. Summer camp, however, is not just for kids.

Do you remember trading things when you were young? It wasn't stressful. In my little suburb in Pittsburgh, we traded baseball cards. We traded a bat for a glove. We traded toy soldiers. There was no stress, just this for that. Children make it simple; they are natural negotiators.

My father always said, "Childhood is an amazing thing; too bad it's wasted on kids." I never looked that quote up, and refuse to do so to this day, many years after my father's premature demise. That phrase is ours—my dad's and mine—even posthumously. He said that phrase a lot, mostly when he was headed to work, and I was off to do something he couldn't do because he had to provide for us. He wasn't bitter about it. It was just a fact. He had his job and responsibility, and I had... well, very little accountability as is often true of us during our early childhood.

Though he used it at other times, summer camp was what mostly triggered my father's favorite childhood phrase. And it stayed with me. So, when I was deep into adulthood, I decided there was only one way to test my father's hypothesis—go to summer camp!

It Started with a Father's Wisdom

The summer of 2008 found me at a camp for those training in the Russian martial art of Systema. The leaders of this style of martial arts offer immersion training every other year at a unique camp in Muskoka, a recreational area about three hours north of Toronto, Canada.

The camp is situated on a lake surrounded by dense forests. It is a place like no other. We woke up each morning and did morning exercises which consisted of calisthenics, walking and breathing, and stretching. We would then have breakfast together in a cafeteria, followed by morning training which was in various self-defense techniques. After lunch, we would head into the woods to learn how to work and live with nature. There were more drills, often with knives. Sometimes we would simply train in the water, learning to be comfortable with moving in the water, which in Northern Ontario was very cold water. After dinner there was night training where we learned to get comfortable dealing with the dark and unknown. And the entire time we were learning with and training with people we did not know.

Here is a caveat about company summer camps. This summer camp is not to be confused with the traditional leadership retreat that many companies schedule annually. In fact, it's completely different. A *Forbes* magazine article titled "Seven Ways to Rethink Your Next Leadership Retreat"[1] points out that all too often the traditional leadership retreat fails in its purpose. According to the article, "Each year, thousands of top managers and board members head to the hills for an annual ritual: the strategic offsite retreat. The purpose of such meetings, of course, is to get away from it all and strategize. To leave behind the distractions and quarterly pressures. To think big about the future."

The article continues, "But all too often, that's not what transpires. Instead, the future gets drowned out by the present. Presentations run over. Social events and the golf outing seem to always get their due. But the time for connecting the dots, brainstorming and open-ended discussion of threats and white space opportunities evaporates. Before you know it, time's up. Once again, the future has been postponed."

Why attend summer camp instead of leadership retreats? It has to do with restoration and replenishment.

I started going at the age of 49 and now, as a grandfather, I continue to go to summer camps to rediscover the child in me that my father always talked about. Last summer, I couldn't find a good camp, so I told my golf instructor down in Los Cabos, Mexico, that we had to create a camp for golf. And we did. I had to show up for two lessons a day, each followed by nine holes. I invited others to my camp, and it was great. After all of these camps, I come back not only refreshed, but stronger, with more clarity, focus, and replenished creative juices. The result? I become a better negotiator and a better leader.

Surrender Control

When you go to summer camp, you give up control to somebody else. What a healthy change for us grown-ups, managerial and executive control freaks. Those of us who are managers, professionals, and executives have a high need for control. We are able to enter a different learning mode when we surrender control.

I remember taking the old FIRO B test, or Fundamental Relations Orientation-Behavior T^2, in the area of human capital, which assessed how someone's personal needs affected their behavior toward other people. Boy, was I off the charts on the need for control. You probably are, too.

Think about how much of growing up involved controlling yourself and others. When I was young, we were graded on control. But when you are in control, you risk having blinders on. And there are many unexpected and chaotic elements you can't always control.

By surrendering control to the summer camp leaders, I was able to relax, learn, and breathe without fearing the loss of control.

Summer camp is organized and managed by the guides and coaches. I didn't need to plan or direct or take charge of things. During the first few days I experienced some control anxiety, which soon passed. I was able to surrender to the process that was radically changing our usual environment and routines. This opened me to new ways of learning and to change.

Discombobulating or Disrupting the Norms

The most important part of the learning process at summer camp is discombobulation or disruption.

- You trade your house for a tent.
- You trade your Porsche for hiking boots.
- You trade your television for a real sunset.
- You trade the urban jungle for the forest.

We studied the process of human change in organizations when I was in graduate school. The concept of "Changing as Three Steps" involves the phases of unfreezing, changing, and refreezing.[3] Referred to as "boot camp," this concept is often attributed to the founder of social psychology, Kurt Lewin. Authors use boot camp as one of the most incredible human change experiences. How do we take a sweet 18-year-old who was taught in church and in school to love others, and train that same sweet child to kill on command? If you watch any movie that offers a legitimate portrait of the boot camp experience such as *Full Metal Jacket* or *An Officer and a Gentleman*, you will quickly see the discombobulation that affects the change. Clothes are taken away. Hair is cut. Wake up time is before dawn at 4 or 5 a.m. That's discombobulation. That's disruption. That creates an environment which makes you receptive and more susceptible to change. It happens at boot camp, and it happens at summer camp. Behaviors are "unfrozen" through discombobulation.

New and Unique Friends

One of the best things about summer camp is making new and different friends. Let's face it. We live in neighborhoods and silos of contained social structures that get narrower as we age. Our circles are frequently restricted to the community in which we live and our workplace. How sad.

At summer camp you meet people from all over the world. Some of them won't like you at first, and you might not like them. You may question their different backgrounds, cultures, experiences, and ways of doing things. Even though it's unsettling and strange, it's healthy. Encountering change, dealing with different people, being exposed to unusual customs and traditions strengthens leaders and makes them more empathetic. They become more experienced with novel conditions and ultimately more skilled when they get back to their workplace and the negotiating table. That's the power of summer camp disruption. Although not as intense as military boot camp, it's equally effective in producing change.

Get Reacquainted with Nature

As we live our lives, we often move from a view of nature as a playground to nature as an inconvenience. In this sad devolvement, we say, "It's raining. I'm going to get wet walking to my car. The forecast says sleet. How am I going to navigate icy roads? The sun is shining bright. Did I remember to bring my sunscreen?" Nature, all too frequently, becomes associated with extra work. It becomes an annoyance.

But at summer camp we roll around in the grass, hide in the dark, train with knives while circling the trees, and find our way back in the dark. Nature was given to us to enjoy, not dominate, manipulate, and whine about. The experience of rediscovering and reconnecting to the nature of your childhood will have a profound effect on you as a leader and negotiator when you return.

Learn to Breathe Again

Our breath patterns are structured around our modern lifestyle. We breathe out of habit. When you shave, you breathe a certain way. Driving in traffic, your breathing pattern often changes to short breaths. When you are under stress, those short breaths continue to be your breathing pattern. When you are tense, you don't breathe as deeply, and this deprives your body of oxygen. Think of taking a deep sigh. I believe sighs are your body's way of saying, "Really?" They prompt you to take stock of what is happening.

At camp, outside where the air is clean and pure, you can relearn how to really breathe. At the Systema camp we breathe—a lot. We practice breathing whether we are doing push-ups or walking across the terrain for miles. This focus on the breath allows us to learn effective ways of breathing according to activity and heightens awareness of when breathing patterns are constrained and less effective.

When you come back from camp, those deep, satisfying breathing patterns will stay with you. They will continue stabilizing and energizing you as you meet life's demands.

Rediscover Your Sense of Smell

Our senses were designed for the woods and the outdoors, and they light up when they are stimulated by nature. Scientists tell us that smell is the oldest of all our senses and is powerfully linked to memory. In our urban lives, our sense of smell is limited to man-made odors and scents that lack the freshness of nature. There are still "smell cues" that exist, though. Office work and negotiation are physical and stressful activities. How healthy is the room you are in? How is the temperature? How is the ventilation? These factors can affect your performance. Often, you are so inside your head that you aren't aware of these factors, yet they affect how your brain performs and, therefore, how you perform. Allowing feelings and sensations about your circumstances as you would in the outdoors is critical. We now know that COVID-19 was spread more easily in poorly ventilated, confined spaces. If your meeting circumstances are uncomfortable, you should stop and see what needs changing. If you are not the host, you should insist on a good environment. If you are the host, you should have set up a comfortable environment. The quality of thinking and discovery are affected by the environment.

Takeaway

I head to summer camp in Northern Ontario every couple of years for a full week. I look forward to turning over control, opening to new ways of learning, partnering with nature, and making new, if sometimes strange, friends. I reawaken my awareness of breathing and re-engage my senses to expand the fullness of life's experiences.

I hope that you find a summer camp for yourself soon and reconnect with your inner child! It will prepare you to be a better leader and a better negotiator. The child within you was an incredible natural negotiator. You will be really impressed with the capabilities of your youthful self.

Go find him or her.

CHAPTER 5

BACK-TO-SCHOOL MENTALITY AND ALWAYS BE TRAINING

> *We learn 10% of what we read, 20% of what we hear, 30% of what we see, 50% of what we see and hear, 70% of what we discuss, 80% of what we experience, 95% of what we teach others.*
> —William Glasser

From a Negotiation to an Education Frame of Mind

An article from the Harvard Graduate School of Education points out that, "Negotiation is about winners and losers, many of us tend to think. In education, the very word 'negotiation' may conjure images of tense and adversarial exchanges…" The authors then go on to point out that there exists a different view of negotiation. They continue "...For those who study the practice of negotiation, it's all about solving complex problems that require the cooperation of others. Negotiation can be positive, constructive, and generative..."[1]

Now that you have gotten in touch with your childhood openness through summer camp, you need to develop a "back-to-school" mentality. You can approach a negotiation like the learning experience it should be. Great negotiations are a process of discovery, similar to what you experience in a class or a school project. Like other students, martial arts students spend all their time training for a confrontation that likely will never happen. We train to defend ourselves for a threat that will hopefully never come. But whether in school or in a dojo, learning, training, and practicing are the keys to being a great negotiator. To get in the learning mode, I find it helpful to adopt a back-to-school mentality. Here are some tips to get in the learning mode.

Every fall, school bells ring, but not for those of us in the workplace. But should they? Should an imaginary bell ring in our heads every fall to boost our productivity and success? Weren't some of our most productive and fun times during the fall semester at school? Weren't we the most energized? The most creative? The most excited? Perhaps that same structure and mentality of returning to school should be incorporated into our post-schoolwork lives.

Developing a regular "back-to-school" mentality through bringing back some fall school rituals will put you into a learning and discovery mode. It will reinvigorate your leadership passion, sharpen your skills, and help you feel that youthful, "anything is possible" energy. The result? You will become a stronger, more engaged leader and negotiator at every level.

Back-to-School Rituals

Shop for new clothes. As the summer came to a close, my mom would take me shopping for school clothes. We weren't poor, but we were definitely lower middle class. We shopped with coupons, mostly at JC Penney where my mother used to work. Nobody knew how to find a sale like my mom. She loved that store. She even named me after James C. Penney— Cash was his middle name. We would get pants, shirts, underwear, socks, and even shoes. My mother would tug at my shirt, adjust my trousers, and argue with the salesperson about fit. As much as I hated trying on all those clothes, it felt great to have brand-new clothes and shoes. New stuff always put a spring in my step.

Having a back-to-school mentality means getting some new threads for yourself. Grab a friend or a loved one and head to the stores. Then get a new head-to-toe outfit. Nothing will empower you as much as walking into the office all decked out in a new suit, shirt, tie, and shoes. That confidence you feel will show from the inside out.

How people dress for a negotiation is interesting. In my younger years, everyone wore suits and ties. You wouldn't think of negotiating a deal without a nice suit or tie if you were a professional. Sometimes, the principals in negotiations would make the point they were the decision maker by wearing something unconventional. One of the best modern ways to show you are in power is to dress down. Principals might choose not to wear socks. Principals might wear jeans and a jacket. What they are showing is that they don't have to care. It can be a real power move.

I was recently called into an all-day mediation in a lawsuit where our company had been sued by the plaintiff's lawyers in California. I was away at the time and had inside and outside counsel working the case. When mediation was suggested by the lawyers, they wanted me to attend. They said the mediator would appreciate having the CEO there for at least the beginning. I happened to be at my home in Cabo San Lucas at the time and told our outside counsel I didn't have a suit to wear. The counsel said, "No worries, wear your beach attire; that will be great." I did, and it had the desired effect that I basically wanted to convey and also that my counsel wanted me to convey. My casual attire conveyed that I was fine and not really worried about the case. We settled for a fraction of the initial demand.

Whether you wear new threads or ones you already own, what you wear affects the other side as well as it affects you. If you feel good, that will come across. I remember choosing the wrong outfit for a negotiation. There was an EEOC (Equal Employment Opportunity Commission) claim against one of my companies for pregnancy discrimination. One of our managers had said, out of concern for the pregnant employee, that maybe she shouldn't travel to our annual meeting.

Nothing horrible, but that wasn't his decision to make. The decision was hers and her doctor's, and he had no business even expressing an opinion. But he was her boss, and he did express this opinion.

The EEOC had offered mediation. I happened to be in the city where the mediation was to take place, so I offered to do it myself. I was visiting clients, so I was wearing a suit. I entered the EEOC offices in the city and immediately noticed I was by far the best-dressed person in the office. This turned out to be unfortunate. I watched the EEOC mediator take in my snappy outfit. I will spare you the details, but the outcome was not as favorable to us as it probably could have been. At one point, the mediator said to me when we were alone, "Look, you are a big, rich company; you can afford to pay her some money. You know she could use it." The merits of the case were not the issue as they should have been. I wore an emblem of wealth expressed by my clothing, and wealth-sharing fit perfectly with the mediator's objective and view of the situation.

Buying school supplies. "You need to sharpen your pencil" was a typical expression in school for needing to do additional work on something. Even though pencils aren't used that much anymore, still one of the most common phrases a buyer will say when they think your price is too high is "sharpen your pencil."

Schools provide a list every year of required supplies, but my mom always went further—beyond the pencils, pens, erasers, and notebooks. She would try to make sure we had as many tools as we needed to succeed. If we couldn't afford something, my mom always figured out a substitute. I remember getting good at sharpening my pencil with a pocketknife because I didn't have a pencil sharpener. (Of course, that was before pocketknives were considered weapons and you couldn't bring them to school.)

Here is an analogy between school preparation and negotiation. As part of your negotiation preparation, examine your tools. Make an inventory of what tools you use every day. Keep track of how often you use each tool. Many tools are apps now. Some of the tools of negotiation are notetaking apps, basic tools like Excel, PowerPoint, and Word. Project management software to keep track of progress on various items is important. And it is not just the tools themselves, but how well you are trained in those tools. I tend to think that your brain is a tool. How well do you take care of yourself to optimize brain function? What are you doing to exercise your mind and body? Note how often you find yourself wishing for a tool you don't have. Check with friends and colleagues about what tools they use. Then get yourself to a store or get online to check out some of the latest tools and improve your toolbox.

I had a client one time watching me negotiate a deal. At one point I took out a pen to make a few notes, and I was surprised when everyone present looked pointedly at my pen. It was a normal office pen you buy in bulk. My client was the CEO of a major public company in Texas. After the meeting, he said, "You need to get yourself a better pen." After we settled his controversy in the seven figures, one of the many gifts he gave me was a Mont Blanc pen. Since then, I have bought several Mont Blanc pens. It is amazing the effect it has when you take out a nice pen. It has an impact on the room. People notice. However, don't bring a Mont Blanc pen to an EEOC negotiation! It does send a definite message of success and wealth.

Most negotiators are proud of their observation skills and notice what others do. In the process of observing, don't forget that similar lenses are aimed at you. Pay attention to your tools. Having the right tools makes you confident, functional, and can convey the messages you want to send. So, as part of getting that back-to-school mentality, get yourself a toolbox and fill it with the tools you need. You'll see just how much your performance will improve as a result.

Get an advisor. At school, we were given an advisor, an assigned person you could talk to if you needed help or advice. Sometimes it was the school counselor. Sometimes it was your homeroom teacher. But whoever was assigned, it was always a person you could confide in and trust about issues, whether you were having trouble with another student, or you just needed some advice about what classes to take. These advisors were a safety valve, provided another perspective and point of view, and acted as a guide.

Having a mentor to talk to about your negotiations is critical. It is so important that I have included an entire chapter regarding the need for this resource. Helpful mentors are invaluable. I could spend many pages discussing the best strategies to get a mentor, but basically you just need to ask someone. Be honest and say that you're looking for a mentor to help you to think about a negotiation, deal, or dispute. Having another perspective is a must. Great mentors will advance your career, no matter what your career stage may be.

I look for people who are 10 to 15 years older than me, and who have advanced professionally beyond my level. I tell them I need help and that I hope to be where they are in a decade or so. I offer to reciprocate in some way, through payment or otherwise. Mentors almost always turn this offer of repayment down, but you should always put it out there.

Look for a successful person who loves talking about their successes and failures. Avoid those who talk only about their successes; you won't learn what you need from them. Remember, if you are training to fight, seeking someone without scars as a mentor won't be helpful. I actively seek out scarred warriors, who are just as I am.

Reading list. School meant assignments and a required reading list. This was a list of assigned books selected for you to read during the school year to enhance your abilities, expand your knowledge base, and generally make you a better person—able to cope and succeed in life.

What a wonderful concept to bring back for those of us stuck in the rut of the daily workday grind. What a wonderful concept to bring to the lives of people in leadership positions. A reading list brings resources with new ideas, inspiration, and links to the thoughts of others. Great negotiators are well-read and interesting liberal-arts-type folks. They have lots to talk about and understand many things because, among other skills, they read a lot.

How do you create a reading list for yourself? It takes a little planning and varies according to your profession. Here are some ideas of how to begin.

○ Commit to reading a magazine like *The Economist* to give you an outside perspective on the U.S.'s businesses and economics.

○ Read some business bestsellers completely out of your field or area of work.

○ Go back in time and taking a fresh look at *The Adventures of Huckleberry Finn*. (One year I read Mark Twain's complete works. That was a great year for my negotiations!)

○ Dig into that Shakespeare play you never finished. You'll be amazed at the Bard's grasp of human foibles and motives.

○ Read at least one article from *The Harvard Business Review* every few months.

○ Check out recommended reading lists online.

○ Consider some titles from the *The Wall Street Journal* or *The New York Times* Best Seller list.

○ The possibilities are endless, and no matter what you select, you will approach your negotiations with a fresh perspective.

Goals. In school, goals are set for you. You are given specific deadlines by which to complete all assignments. These are firm deadlines often with significant consequences for failure to hit those targets. Sometimes there is a little flexibility, but it doesn't last. I once overheard a graduate student in an accounting course ask for an extension on a project, then on a paper, and then on a test. I remember the accounting professor first giving him some latitude, but then eventually warning him, "You do understand that there is an end to these extensions, and that eventually, you have to hand in the work."

We all have projects that can drag on longer than anticipated. Why not do what they did back in school? Adopt a deadline approach. Set specific timeframes for completing your goals and stick to them. You will maintain better discipline if you know that you'll get an "incomplete" or failing grade if you don't finish the tasks by a specific date. Ask a colleague or family member to hold you accountable. You will be surprised how a deadline can focus you and improve your productivity. This deadline mentality will be especially valuable as you move through the various challenging stages of a negotiation.

For every negotiation, and in teaching my negotiation class, I do a preview and review for every meeting or exchange. I am shocked at how many people, including lawyers, show up to negotiations and "wing it." Maybe they use the document or a checklist to remind them of material matters, but real planning doesn't exist. An example of a template I use is in the appendix of this book. After the negotiation session, meeting, or exchange, I write a reflection. Think of it as preparing for class and making notes after class. I use these notes to help me improve my negotiating skills in general as well as to track where a deal or dispute is heading. I call it Preview/Review.

Students who have taken my class know that for every class they will be doing a preview and a review. I do it myself to lead by example.

Grades. One of the easiest reminders that you are a student is grades. As a student, you are graded on everything you do. You take a quiz, you get a grade. You take mid-terms, you get a grade. Final exam means a grade. It is relentless, and it is continuous.

Once we're out of school, what do we do in the workplace and our professional lives to evaluate how we're doing? Uh, annual performance reviews? Seriously, after you become accustomed to feedback in the form of grades every week, every mid-term, every semester, you take a job and get a vague annual review instead of grades. It's no wonder employees look quizzically at their managers after performance reviews and wonder how they are really doing.

If you are a manager, start giving more feedback. If you are an employee, start asking for more feedback. You can even admit that you are conditioned to being graded regularly, and you expect that kind of specificity in performance rating. Never wonder how you are doing. Push for feedback until you get it. Whatever level of organizational responsibility you have, frequent grades and frequent feedback on performance will help accelerate your success path.

You could always learn to evaluate yourself. I ask my students to define negotiation success, and they develop these definitions throughout the semester. Then, they use these developing definitions to help them evaluate their performance. Using defined measures for success, they get weekly feedback on their negotiation work. What are you doing to honestly evaluate your success in your negotiations? Having a specific evaluation system is essential.

Friends. A new school year always brought with it new friends—and unfortunately new enemies. As you move through your educational life and into your professional one, you will come to realize that enemies can play a positive role. They can bring us challenges that will make us stronger, more effective, more likely to win more often. We hone our negotiating skills through dealing with enemies, just as martial artists do with their opponents.

Much of our success in work and in life is determined by our social skills. In negotiations, these soft skills are critical. We all need to navigate friends, enemies, and people who couldn't care less about us. The ability to navigate all different types of people at all different levels will only improve with practice. This will add an important skill to your professional negotiation toolbox.

When I was a young lawyer at Union Pacific Railroad, I was fairly intense. A wise advisor, the assistant vice president of law, a man who had fought at the Battle of the Bulge in World War II, told me to lighten up a little. He instructed me that 85 percent of my success would be based on how well I got along with others. Three decades after getting that advice, I can tell you that it was right on the mark.

Enhancing social skills is a foundation for good interactions with people. When people feel good about their interactions, they are more likely to agree and cooperate. This will make them more inclined to reach compatible conclusions. Get yourself into some new social situations and sharpen those critical social skills that will advance your negotiation and career success.

In the martial arts, all of these factors are in play. When you join a dojo, you get a new uniform and a white belt. You have a sensei or instructor to guide your way. You train and train and train. You are evaluated and given a new belt as you master material. You buy tapes and books to advance your education. Your goal is to get a black belt. So the back-to-school mentality applies equally to martial arts and negotiating; for clothes, goals, grades, reading, learning, and forming new friendships all come into play.

Takeaway

Whatever time of year, you can pretend it is mid-August, and school bells will soon be ringing. It's time to get yourself some new threads, think about what you are wearing, update and upgrade your tools, find yourself a new mentor, create and execute on a reading list, set yourself some goals, grade yourself relentlessly and force others to grade you, too, and challenge yourself socially.

A back-to-school mentality will cause you to rejuvenate and re-energize your negotiation and leadership skills. Hurry, the bell is getting ready to ring!

CHAPTER 6

NEGOTIATORS ARE OFTEN ROAD WARRIORS

Be your brand...
When you are excellent you become unforgettable.

—Oprah Winfrey

The Road Warrior Life

I have spent almost four decades as a deal-making Road Warrior. This includes traveling as a corporate lawyer, as an entrepreneur, and as a CEO flying all over the country and the world to enter into a wide variety of negotiations. The issue of travel brings forth questions about the impact of "home turf," knowledge and awareness of "the terrain," and other logistical issues.

These types of issues are very relevant in the world of martial arts and conflict generally. In sports contests we talk about the "home field advantage." Sun Tzu, a 5th-6th century BC Chinese military strategist and philosopher, talks about the importance of "terrain." I have participated in martial arts seminars that focused on footing. When we train in the martial arts, we most often train in nice martial arts dojos, with mats to protect us, if and when we fall to the floor. We train at convenient times. We train in comfortable clothing. We train when we feel well and don't train when we don't feel well. We train in well-lit studios. We train with fellow students. We train face to face. They don't mean us harm.

But the real-world conflict and attacks, if and when they happen, are not on our terms. I was walking back from a dinner to my hotel in Los Angeles on Century Boulevard and suddenly noticed three people following me. I felt they were stalking me (I am confident they were). I was tired. It was dark. I was full, having eaten a large meal. I was in a suit with dress shoes. And they were behind me. I was walking on concrete. There was no one else around me. I sensed they meant me harm.

But when I trained in Systema, I trained in the dark in Canada. I trained in perceiving whether people meant me harm. I trained on terrain that was uneven. I trained in regular clothes. I got training from people who had been in real combat situations. So, I knew not to run. That is what "prey" does, after all. I knew to act like I didn't have a care in the world. I let them know I was aware but fine. I exuded a non-confrontational confidence that caused them to break off from me. And that is not my only such experience traveling. Traveling on business, like most traveling, is a risk, and it is stressful.

Lessons to Become a Successful Road Warrior

All of this traveling may have taken its toll, but it has also provided me with some invaluable lessons. I would like to share them with you, as a way of preparing you for being a successful Road Warrior in deal-making and negotiating adventures. I will include some lessons I learned in 36 years of traveling for negotiations, and in the process share some thoughts on the advantages of making these trips. I'll give some good tips on how travel can provide an edge in negotiating.

Stay in the same hotel each time you visit a city. The number one downside of traveling on business is that you are away from your family and friends. However, by staying in the same hotel you will be able to satisfy the natural need for familiar contact, security, and companionship. Here's an example of how that plays out. I began my career as a corporate attorney at Union Pacific Railroad in 1985. I was doing corporate law, primarily mergers and acquisitions. M&A attorneys are heavy travelers. In just a few years, I became responsible for the airfreight company Union Pacific had acquired with the Missouri Pacific Railroad purchase. The airfreight company had substantial operations in California, especially Los Angeles.

Today, 36 years later, I still stay at the same hotel when traveling to Los Angeles. Some of the same hotel employees I met back in 1985 are still there. Several years ago, I was having a drink at the bar. One of the bartenders said, "You've been coming here for many years." I replied, "You've been working here for many years." We both laughed. It isn't home, but by staying in this hotel consistently whenever I'm in L.A., I feel that I'm around people I have known for a long time. I sleep better there, and a good night's sleep on the road is both important and all too often rare.

Get out of your hotel for meals. Ask the concierge or front desk person to recommend eateries the locals like. Take advantage of being in a different place. Get a sense of the local color while away from home. The traveling dealmaker lifestyle takes a physical toll. Reward yourself. Eating at a local hangout will give you not only the flavors of the meal, but also of the local community and culture. We live in a wonderful and diverse world—don't confine yourself to conference rooms, negotiating tables, and hotel restaurants and rooms. But also ask where it is safe and where it is not.

Explore your surroundings. Get up early and take a walk after you have made certain that you're in a safe area. On a recent business trip to Florida, I got up and walked on the boardwalk along the ocean. I even watched the sunrise. I know this can be difficult because such trips often include long, heavy dinners and early morning meetings. But find time for yourself and get out into the open air. You will feel better, and you will be more attentive and effective in your business activities. These types of activities can help you with finding common interests and making small talk at the beginning or during breaks in your negotiations.

I remember as a young lawyer when I worked on the acquisition of Overnight Transportation in Richmond, Virginia.

I took a stroll and saw there was a lot of remodeling activity in the neighborhood where I was staying. I mentioned to the counterparty representatives that I had noticed quite a bit of home remodeling in the area. The VP in charge of the deal immediately corrected me and said, "Cash, we don't remodel here in Richmond; we restore." That comment reminded me to respect the pride they had in their city, its culture and history. This also applied to their company, giving me insight into how to approach them during negotiations.

Visit someplace historic. Virtually every location you visit for business has a historic site worth seeing. Take time to find out what it is and go see it. Recently, I was in Atlanta, and during a break in negotiation sessions, I visited the Civil War battlefield at Kennesaw Mountain. I had never visited a Civil War museum in the South. Obviously, the Southern perspective on this period of American history is very different from what I was taught in elementary and high school in the North. After I watched the movie in that Southern museum, I wasn't quite sure that the North won the Civil War. Talk about a new perspective! Take advantage of all the new perspectives available when you travel and bring that freshness and newness back into the meeting room.

Understanding the "home turf" of your counterparty can be invaluable in helping you reach agreement. As I have said, negotiations are rich social engagements and understanding your counterparty is critical. We were in town trying to buy a small company. Imagine if I had said, "Didn't General Sherman spend some time here?" Mentioning the Union general whose victories brought great destruction to the South would not only have destroyed any goodwill, it probably would have destroyed any hope of a deal.

Exercise, exercise, exercise. No matter what hotel I stay in, I am always amazed at how few people use the gym. If you want to survive as a Road Warrior, making time to exercise is the most important thing you can do for yourself. Just start walking on the treadmill, get on an elliptical, lift some weights, play with a medicine ball, stretch. Do something that involves your whole body for 30 minutes. You will live longer and be more engaged and engaging in your negotiation meetings.

Eat a healthy meal every night. Eating on the road is difficult because you are on an expense account and have way too many dining choices. I am mostly a pescatarian and vegetarian, and that helps me avoid those monstrous steak dinners. By limiting yourself to specific foods you can avoid fat, carbs, and other less healthy choices and portions. After a little practice, you soon won't be tempted by all those rich menu items. Your mind will be clearer, and you won't have to deal with indigestion, making you more alert during negotiations.

Me and My Monk at 37,000 Feet

Engage with fellow travelers. Whether on a flight, at a restaurant, in a hotel, or at the bar, get outside your comfort zone and meet somebody. You never know what you might learn from a fellow Road Warrior. One night I was taking a flight from Dallas to Hartford to negotiate a new contract with a major aerospace company. Just as I was settling into my seat, a man dressed in a saffron and maroon robe, with a clean-shaven head, sat down in the seat next to mine. We both looked at one another but we didn't speak. As the flight progressed, I drank wine and watched a James Bond movie. My fellow passenger the monk read Sanskrit and meditated. I left him alone.

Near the end of the trip, I turned to him and asked, "Are you a monk?"

He smiled broadly. "Yes I am. Are you?"

"What do you think?" I replied.

"I think you are," he said.

"Where are you going?" I asked.

"To Smith College to teach," he said.

"What will you teach?" I asked further.

"Compassion and Death," he told me.

I then asked him, "What is the most important thing to understand about death?"

"That it is natural," he answered.

He then went on to explain that because we no longer live near our parents and grandparents, we lose sight of how death is a natural process. Because people commonly try to avoid pain, we avoid being a part of the dying process.

I said, "So we experience death as if it was a show on-demand—out of sight, out of mind."

"Yes," he said.

I told him instead of studying death and dying, I was still learning to live and maybe if he ever wanted a co-teacher, I could teach life, and he could teach death.

He considered it for a moment, smiled again, and grasped my shoulder. Then we parted ways. The next day at the end of a Chinese lunch with colleagues and members of our counterparty, I got a fortune cookie that said, "Soon you will achieve perfection." I know it was from my monk. I shared the story with all at lunch, and it was one of those things that brought everyone closer.

Takeaway

Life as a Road Warrior is a tough life. But deals and sales, as I remind folks, don't come to you. You have to go get them. To keep your sanity and your soul, sleep at familiar hotels, engage with your environment, explore local attractions, jump on a treadmill, and manage your diet. Each of these activities provides you with stories to share with counterparties and lessons on the local culture and attitudes. Collecting these stories and experiences will assist you in your negotiations. Most importantly, make new friends. Interact with strangers—the stranger the better. Who knows, you may even get blessed by a monk.

Travel safely, my fellow Road Warriors!

CHAPTER 7

A MENTOR IS A MUST

The mind is not a vessel that needs filling,
but wood that needs igniting.

—Plutarch

Primacy

Just like your first job, your first negotiation is one that you
will never forget. Scientists call this first-time experience "primacy." Primacy is the special impact of what comes first.
That's exactly what happens when you get your first mentor.
First mentors are like first loves. You never forget them. You
never forget those first years of guidance and the feeling of
being taken under somebody's wing; somebody who teaches
you to fly—to soar.

Mentors are like a sensei. They are your teacher. I remember vividly all the lessons from my many senseis over the years.

Those lessons came in many forms, but each teacher provides you with tweaks to your physical movement, tips for your day-to-day actions, and proverbs for your life. So much of your life is impacted by your sensei. In the business world, these senseis are invaluable, and we call them mentors.

My first mentor, Forrest Krutter, former general counsel and secretary to Berkshire Hathaway, was one of the most intelligent people I have ever met. He was my first mentor when we worked together at Union Pacific Railroad in Omaha, Nebraska. He was one of those rare math and engineering types who went to law school. As best I can recall, he had earned a BS in economics and a master's in engineering from Massachusetts Institute of Technology, both in the same year. That wasn't enough for him. He entered Harvard Law School and graduated with a law degree. He had completed all these degrees by 24 years of age. Forrest followed the legacy set down by brilliant railroad lawyers whose ranks included Clarence Darrow, Daniel Webster, and Abraham Lincoln.

That First Acquisition

Forrest wasn't my boss. In fact, he was only a few years older than me. But he became my guide during the single year we worked together on the acquisition of Overnight Transportation, the largest transportation acquisition in history at the time. For this, we needed antitrust approval from the Interstate Commerce Commission. It was a massive undertaking. We virtually lived together for an entire year, working that transaction and getting approval.

It was a year I will never forget. I learned many of my most important professional lessons during that year.

In the *Negotiable Guide for Mentors*, the authors point out that, "Less-experienced negotiators frequently take a narrow view of negotiation, often overwhelmingly focused on their desired deal terms. Experienced and effective dealmakers tend to have a broader view of bargaining dynamics, including different 'dramas' that can be harnessed or could pose threats, such as the negotiating process itself as well as the impact of other people who might not appear directly at the table."[1]

Lessons I Learned

So, what did I learn from my brilliant first mentor? The most profound lesson can be summarized as "Succinct is the secret of deep analysis."

I don't remember whether Forrest liked two-page or three-page memoranda, but I do remember that he judged how much you analyzed something by how concise you could be. He wasn't looking for short because he didn't want to read, but because he knew that the tighter your writing was, the closer to the heart of the issue you were and the more clearly you could express it.

This is especially critical when you are prepping for any negotiation. I ask for a preview and review from my students in negotiation class. I want to know what their plan is for the upcoming negotiation, and afterward I ask for their reflections on what happened in their negotiation. I think they are always shocked when I tell them that I only want a page or two for each, the preview and the review. A careful analysis written down is a powerful tool in making your strategy successful.

This is "getting to the core" and it happens in two parts, Forrest taught me. The first part is the document itself. It should be clean, deep, and accurate. It must be an effective analysis and summary of the issues.

The second part is the "kernel" within the document. The kernel is one or two key sentences that summarize the objective or point of the document in such a way that the reader can easily pluck the essence from it. Forrest explained, "You need to give them advice, not in conceptual terms, but a rule or the simple principle that can guide their conduct in the matter." And so, Forrest got me in the habit of making sure there were one or two sentences the reader could take and paste to the side of their desk.

The kernel that would guide negotiations came from succinct statements, the result of deep analysis. This provides principles useful throughout negotiation that help you to keep your eye on the objectives.

There is No Such Thing as a Draft

One of the most important skills, maybe a lost art in today's world of emails and texts, is drafting the business memorandum. I remember one of my first assignments from Forrest involved research on an issue, then committing that research to a memo to offer the client advice on an aspect of the deal.

He asked me for a draft. When I heard the word "draft" I immediately associated it with something that was a try. I associated it with a first effort. So I gave him a draft, roughed out and not necessarily focused on perfection. What a mistake on my part. Forrest threw a fit and made a tremendous fuss about it. He pointed out even the smallest typo and some minor grammar mistakes. After suffering many kind but firm reviews from him, I finally said, "It's only a draft. You said you wanted a draft." Forrest smiled at me and said, ''There is no such thing as a draft. You put your name on it and it leaves your office; it is not a draft. It is you, and it is your best work."

I learned an important lesson from this. During any negotiation, there is a vast amount of correspondence, a large number of reports, analyses, and written scenarios. Every one of them must be perfect before it leaves your control. Every "draft" must be crafted and presented as if it were the final document. It must be your best work. This attention to detail is a valuable habit that will give you the edge in your negotiating interactions.

The "Never Stop Learning" Principle in Negotiations

Working with Forrest, I learned many things each day. He managed in a way that always had me looking things up to keep pace with him, and this was well before the internet and Google. This research took time and effort. But this was integral to Forrest's way of life. It was his motto—never stop learning.

In negotiations, the "never stop learning" principle can make the difference between a bad deal and a good one. It can be the factor between a good deal and a great one. Learning is now firmly part of my negotiation toolbox. My latest learning is in the area of language and culture because I do so many international negotiations. Virtually every counterparty from another country appreciates you making an effort to understand their culture and their country. I use multiple apps for the language aspect, including Duolingo.

I was negotiating with a team from a major Japanese company. I like F1 racing, and I have a box in Austin. I knew there was a track in Japan and studied up on the track, which is in Suzuka. I bought tickets and arranged a trip to host them at their own track. Some had not been there even though they lived in Japan. It was a great occasion to build trust and rapport. I worked on some key Japanese phrases and studied a bit on the Shinto religion and how it had intertwined to some degree with Buddhism. I asked them about this. They not only explained it to me but took me to a Shinto shrine after the race and showed me how to pray. This was a breakthrough in the area of trust and a fascinating learning experience I will never forget.

"On the Shoulders of Giants"

Good mentors fulfill the concept of standing "on the shoulders of giants." In the article "10 Reasons Why a Mentor is a Must," *Inc. Magazine*[2] lists the top three benefits mentors provide:

1. "Mentors provide information and knowledge. As Benjamin Franklin said, 'Tell me and I forget, teach me and I may remember, involve me and I learn.'
2. "Mentors can see where we need to improve when we often cannot. Moviemaker George Lucas noted, 'Mentors have a way of seeing more of our faults than we would like. It's the only way we grow.' They will always be brutally honest with you and tell you exactly how it is rather than downplay any weaknesses they see in you.
3. "Mentors find ways to stimulate our personal and professional growth. Another famous movie director explained, 'The delicate balance of mentoring someone is not creating them in your own image, but allowing them to create themselves.' My mentor would often pose questions for me to think about and ask me to come back with answers later."

Get a Mentor

Mentorships are important to our future. We live in a world with 71 million Boomers, the generation born between 1946 and 1964; over 60 million GenXers born between 1965 and 1980; and 72 million echo Boomers (also known as Millennials) born between 1981 and 1996. All these generations are now interacting in business and industry.

Boomers need to reach across the GenXers and help the Millennials to accelerate their learning, and to increase their institutional and negotiation knowledge. Sadly, we are not seeing that now. We are seeing what appears to be almost "age warfare." Some Millennials say condescendingly, "OK, Boomer" as a way to classify and dismiss them, and some Boomers think that Millennials are lazy gamers. Imagine if these generations helped and mentored each other, instead of being adversarial. Wisdom and experience could be transmitted to benefit individuals and companies.

Getting a mentor is an essential step toward expanding your skills and abilities in negotiation. Companies, organizations, and institutions need to facilitate mentor relationships. This could be particularly beneficial across generations.

Takeaway

For the first year of my career, a young Forrest Krutter was my mentor, and his teachings were foundational for my career and my approach to deal making. His greatness was evident as he taught me to write a "draft-free" memorandum that was concise, got to the heart of the matter, and had actionable advice. His humility and respect for others were exemplary.

Most importantly, Forrest had a learning mentality. It wasn't a surprise to me when Warren Buffett, who had his choice of any lawyer in the world, picked Forrest to be his general counsel.

My advice is for experienced negotiators to get into a mentor relationship. Share your knowledge and wisdom. Advance someone's progress.

It's good for the negotiation process. It's good for organizations. It's good for your soul. And we need it now more than ever.

CHAPTER 8

THE ART AND SCIENCE
OF MEMORY

*Science and technology revolutionize our
lives, but memory, tradition,
and myth frame our response.*
—Arthur M. Schlesinger

Mental Athletes

Chester Santos is the 2008 USA Memory Champion and
a world-renowned expert on memory techniques. He is
a mental athlete. Chester has memorized remarkable
things like the names of every single member of Congress,
complete with their party affiliation, their district, the com-
mittees on which they serve, and more. But that's not all.
Chester can memorize the names of two hundred people
he has just met.

But Chester will also tell you that he can't remember a thing if he isn't really focused on it in the first place. And that's one of the secrets of memory champions—intensive focus to the point that they engage all their senses, use repetition, and make associations. Ultimately, they can use these techniques to perform astounding acts.

Why is Chester's memory part of a book on negotiation? Because memory is a critical component of a negotiator's skill set. It is one of the most important among cognitive skills and can be used effectively during any negotiation. A savvy negotiator can enhance these memory skills and use them to advantage during the most simple or complex negotiation.

Theory of Mind

The Modern Language Association says that "Negotiating encompasses a range of communicative acts that human beings perform when they seek agreement in the face of conflicting views on something important, such as the value of material or immaterial goods."[1] Memory is a significant player in those acts of communication. Negotiation is a socially rich engagement. When you settle into a room, or engage virtually via Zoom or Teams, or engage in a phone conversation, words and ideas start to fly. Being able to quickly remember who said what puts you in an optimal position to respond. When the negotiation gets heated, as it often does, people are speaking too quickly and spontaneously to capture it in notes. Your ability to think on your feet, remember what who said what, when, and in which context gives you an edge in negotiation.

Memory as a Cognitive Skill

Start with remembering a person's name. How important is remembering someone's name? Perhaps the greatest and best-known teacher of soft skills was Dale Carnegie. He said, "Remember that a person's name is to that person the sweetest and most important sound in any language."[2] This is one of Carnegie's top tips. It's a critical key to getting people to be receptive to you. It is also the key to engaging with others. But be honest with yourself. How often do you ask someone their name and then just 10-15 minutes later think, "What did they say their name was?"

Memory is a cognitive skill that can be developed and honed. Successful negotiators keep up training in essential skills, including remembering. I've been training with Chester Santos since 2011, and it's dramatically upped my game. I did this during my 50s, and my memory is better today than it was earlier in my life. In the foreword that I wrote for Santos' book, *Mastering Memory: Techniques to Turn Your Brain from a Sieve to a Sponge*[3], I used this example. My team was meeting with five representatives from a Fortune 500 company, seeking a contract to be their supplier. As each representative from a different business division made their points, my team members kept furiously taking notes and glancing up and down. I maintained eye contact throughout, using methods I'd learned from Santos to "record" key points and my solutions mentally. When they finished, I responded for my team, reciting all their issues and my solutions. Their jaws dropped, and they asked if I had written notes on my hands. Showing them my blank palms, I said, "No, I just listened. We listen to our customers." Needless to say, we won the contract.

Start with Remembering Names

To build up your memory skills, one of the best places to begin is with people's names. To remember someone's name, first focus on it when you are being introduced. Take in all of that person's features that make them unique and associate those features with their name. Perhaps the person you are being introduced to has a beard. Associate their name with their beard. Perhaps they have curly hair; associate their name with curls. Perhaps the person resembles someone you already know with the same name. That's another valuable association. Whatever characteristic of the person strikes you, apply the same rule. Deliberately make an association of their name with that characteristic.

When you are being introduced, it is important to repeat the name of the person back. Repetition helps fix the name in your memory. And fixing the name in memory is your goal. The party who puts forth that first memory-learning effort to remember people's names is exactly the type of person who has mastered one of the key cognitive skills for an effective and successful negotiation.

Paying Attention is for Winners

I consider paying attention a soft skill. Some people seem to be good at it, and others are not. Even those of us who work on paying attention are challenged at times. But the sheer skill of paying attention can help you anticipate the other party's moves, so it becomes a valuable tool. That is because when you are paying attention, you are more likely to be observant of your counterparty and be less focused on yourself.

Consider this analogy. When you study martial arts, whether it be Karate, Jiu Jitsu, Iaido, Systema, or any other martial art, you don't have the luxury of writing techniques down as you learn them. The techniques are taught verbally as they have been passed down through centuries of culture. It is part of the tradition. You pay close attention to the spoken instructions, and then you perform the technique. You repeat this process over and over again, until you have memorized it and can recite it back to the teacher. The next level of learning that is common with these unwritten techniques, at least in a dojo, is for you to teach it to a junior student. When you are required to teach it to another student, you must have reached a very high level of absorption. You are paying close attention. Nothing escapes your notice. You note and remember everything. And the stakes for not paying attention and remembering are very high in martial arts. You can get seriously injured if your attention wavers. So, knowing that you have to teach the technique accurately to someone else puts even greater emphasis on your attention and concentration. If you do not learn properly, you cannot teach properly.

Getting in "The Zone"

There is an attention zone in which you are maximally focused, and through practice, you find that attention zone. And you want to stay in it. To a martial artist, getting into "the zone" means being in the moment. If you are truly in the moment, your senses are heightened. You notice everything. You miss nothing. In "the zone," everything moves in slow motion. You take everything in. It's like a motion picture where you see the film frame by frame. This acute attention allows you to see things that others don't see.

When I am training deeply in the martial arts, all of motion seems to slow down for me. I can see a bird's wings flap like they are in slow motion; this is because I have been focusing totally on their motion. For a negotiator, reaching that level of attention is a powerful skill. People seem different to you. Your level of engagement with them is enhanced. You sense their motivation and, as a result, perhaps their next statement or "move." As you are more in touch with them, they may sense this as well. Your higher level of engagement might also lift them to this higher level. You, and possibly they, see everything. You miss nothing. And you remember it all. You notice all of their movements. Like a poker player, you can learn their "tells," the subtle motions that give them away.

In response to this way of remembering, people often wonder, "Why don't you just take notes?" The problem with taking notes during a human interaction is that it can actually be a distraction, especially at the negotiating table. To take notes you have to stop participating and look down to write. You break eye contact. Your attention is diverted to the page in front of you and not to the people around you, to the signals they are sending. By taking notes, you run the very real risk of missing something vital, however small, to the negotiation.

Negotiations and other business meetings are not like classes in school. At school, you are being presented with information. It is understood that you will take notes during the lecture. Good professors will even watch as a class takes notes, and time their cadence to the rhythm of those who are following along. Instructors will pause to make sure you have entered every point into your notes that they have made, so you can incorporate it into your studies and recite it back on an exam. Good luck with this during a negotiation. Just when you are about to write something down, several things may be mentioned that you will miss, or the other party may nod, grimace, or let down their guard, and you will miss that too.

I competed in the USA Memory Championship in April 2017. There were four events. The first event was how many random numbers you could remember. The second event was whether and how quickly you could remember a deck of cards. The third event was how many names you could remember, and the fourth was memorizing a poem. It was in Harrisburg. I will never forget the preparation I did with Chester Santos. *CBS News Sunday Morning* show filmed some of my preparation, although it hasn't aired yet. The concentration and focus required for these events is hard to describe. And please consider, I competed at the age of 59 (there was only one person older than me; Dr. Kay, whom I acknowledge in this book). I was able, at the age of 59, to memorize a randomly shuffled deck of cards in less than five minutes. I was only one of twelve competitors in the National Championship who was able to do it.

Do I have a naturally great memory? No. Are adults approaching 60 years old known to be memory competitors? Absolutely not. But learning to be in that moment and focus is what allowed me to accomplish these memory feats. This is a powerful skill that I have carried over into negotiations. It is something that you can and should do also.

Takeaway: A Strong Memory = A Negotiating Edge

Paying attention, focus, and memory are core negotiating-related soft skills. Work on those core negotiating skills. Learn the names, personalities, roles, and idiosyncrasies of the people on the other side of the negotiation. By using creative imagery, get your right brain into the game to "blow away" not only your own team members, but the other negotiating team as well. They will be amazed by your seemingly photographic memory and sharp eye. If you feel the need to have a pencil and paper in front of you to show respect, you can do that, but your success will be far greater if you don't look down too often to take notes. I have tried this no-notes technique in several key negotiations. In each case, I was asked how I remembered everything. I simply said I pay attention.

CHAPTER 9

LISTENING

*"I do not like green eggs and ham. I do not
like them, Sam-I-Am."*
—Dr. Seuss, Green Eggs and Ham

Learning to Pivot from "No!"

What is the first word you remember? It might be "no." The
word "no" is often etched deeply in our psyches as something
to fear. The source of fear arises from the classical condition-
ing that accompanies the spoken word, "no." When we are
young, "no" can accompany a slap, a spanking, a nasty expression from a parent or teacher, or a strong negative tone. The
word "no" can also bring back memories of being deprived
of a desired object.

The word can take us back to our past, impact our present,
and even affect our future. "No" is a powerful word. It's a

word worthy of some reflection, especially if you have any involvement in sales or negotiation. Never forget the power of "no."

The role of "no" in your psyche as it impacts personal and professional life bears examination. Here are some questions to begin this self-study:

How can you learn not to fear the word "no"?

How can you learn not to ignore it?

How can you listen past the negative of "no"?

How can you start a dialogue and ask about its meanings?

How can you learn to understand the real reason behind a "no"?

How can you, through that understanding, achieve your goals?

Green Eggs and Ham was my First Sales Manual

If you had a good childhood, your family probably had Dr. Seuss's books on bookshelves somewhere. Maybe you enjoyed *The Cat in the Hat*. Perhaps you liked *Hop on Pop*. My favorite was, and will always be, *Green Eggs and Ham*.[1] I may not have recognized it as a book about sales then, or the main character, Sam-I-Am, as a salesperson, even though I was a budding salesman myself. Still in grade school, I would get up every morning before dawn and deliver the *Pittsburgh Post-Gazette* at 5:30 am, hours before school. By the tender age of 11, I was a door-to-door salesman, pushing the Sunday and holiday editions of the paper and seeking to expand my route. I can still smell the newsprint.

Even though I may not have seen Sam-I-Am as a salesman back then, I surely see Sam-I-Am as a salesman now. And I am not the only one who has recognized this parallel. Some sales experts view the story as a lesson in persistence and ultimate reward, because no matter how many times the prospect protests "I do not like green eggs and ham. I do not like them, Sam-I-Am," eventually, the green eggs and ham are eaten and even enjoyed by the target.

What's even more remarkable is that the sale is made with only 50 words—repeated endlessly—the result of a bet between Dr. Seuss and his publisher. The $50 bet that turned into an 8-million-copy best seller!

In 1960 Bennett Cerf, the co-founder of Random House, wagered Dr. Seuss $50 to write a book using only fifty or fewer distinct words. The result was *Green Eggs and Ham* which has sold 8 million copies to date and is the top-selling Dr. Seuss book of all time!

Sam-I-Am is a Lousy Listener

Despite his persistence, Sam-I-Am is a lousy listener. All he does is simply push his product, green eggs and ham, over and over again in a different way. The target, wanting to never hear from Sam again, finally says, "Sam! If you let me be, I will try them. You will see." This capitulation comes after the target is offered green eggs and ham in many different ways: here or there, with a mouse, in a house, with a fox, in a box, on a train, in a car, in a tree, and in the dark.

It is a great read and is consistently ranked as one of the top children's stories of all time.

But despite its huge success, *Green Eggs and Ham* is a lousy lesson in listening, sales, and negotiation. Not once does Sam-I-Am ask the simple question, "What don't you like about green eggs and ham?" Not once is there any effort on the part of Sam-I-Am to ask and then listen. Instead, his repeated response to rejection is simply another pitch.

As I reflect on my childhood experiences, I think I modeled Sam-I-Am. I remember being called persistent even after having doors closed in my face, in my attempts trying to sell holiday editions of the *Pittsburgh Post-Gazette*. We were supposed to use the holiday editions to try and get regular subscribers for the daily newspaper. It is sad that door-to-door selling doesn't exist much anymore. It was a great training ground.

Green Eggs and Ham 2.0

Imagine if Sam-I-Am had asked questions instead of just pushing. I think it would be a fun project to rewrite *Green Eggs and Ham* and recast Sam-I-Am, so that when he first asks, "Do you like green eggs and ham?" and the prospect says, "I do not like them, Sam-I-Am, I do not like green eggs and ham," Sam-I-Am listens. Then he seeks to understand why and says, "You do not like green eggs and ham? Which is the worst, the green eggs or the ham?" He could go on to inquire "Is it the color green? Are you a vegetarian?"

So many questions could be asked to discover a solution or path forward. I think it would be great to show the character trying to learn more about the tastes and preferences and desires of his counterparty. I think it would be great to show the character listening carefully and thoughtfully to the answers. And I think it would be great to show how the character changes up his pitch to incorporate what he heard when he listened to his prospect. Now that, I think, would make a great children's book. It would teach listening skills.

You may fairly point out that Sam-I-Am is asking questions; therefore, it is important to make a distinction between two types of questions. Early in my career, I was trained in sales. In classical, needs-satisfaction sales training there are two types of questions. They are generally referred to as "open probes" and "closed probes." If you are a lawyer or just watch lots of crime or legal shows, you will recognize that these types of questions are used differently. One type is what lawyers will ask their own witness; the other type they use for cross examination. Open probes, as the name implies, are open-ended questions, such as "What did you do next?" "Why did you go to the store?" "How are you?" "Where do you live?"

In general, people use open probes to find opportunities and closed probes to identify needs. In salesperson speak, we are looking for needs that our solution can satisfy. But doesn't that sound like negotiating? When you negotiate, you are doing some form of selling. You are selling your "position" or you are selling to solve your counterparty's needs in a way that also gets you or your client what they want. Whether or not you understand this about the professional sales process will impact your negotiating success.

People use closed probes to better understand the potential need. Closed probes are often questions that only call for a yes or no answer. They are also commonly questions that are only offered as multiple choice and often there are only two choices—this or that. Closed probes raise tension while open probes tend to lower tension.

Reach into your own database of experiences. How do you feel when someone says to you, "Hi Sarah, how are you doing?" This is clearly an open probe question. You are probably fine with that question and feel you can answer it however you want. But suppose I say, "Sarah, are you prepared or not for the meeting?" You might like to explain why you aren't prepared. But I have forced you to say "yes" or "no." Watch a cross examination on TV or in a movie. You will notice that the closed probe questions are putting pressure on the witness or defendant. These types of questions are designed to force an answer favorable to the lawyer doing the cross examination.

So Sam-I-Am is asking questions, but what kind of questions are they when he asks, "Would you like it here or there?" "Would you like it with a fox?" All of the questions are pressuring questions and not once does he use a nice, permissive, open-probe question. As soon as someone tells you they don't like green eggs and ham, your next question shouldn't be, "Do you want them here or there?" Your next question should be to understand why. "Why don't you like green eggs and ham?" This open probe will lead to a solution.

We all have run into brick walls in a negotiation, and learning to pivot from "no" is an essential negotiation skill. To pivot from "no," I really like asking "why." The "why" question is a perfect and commonly used open probe. It allows the counterparty to take a path they want to take in answering. It is unconfining and should open up additional paths. But this will not always be the case, and other techniques will be necessary.

Use a Technique from Parent-Child Negotiations to Pivot from "No"

A company I was representing had received an investment, and things hadn't gone according to plan. As a result, the company needed more money. My client from the company and I sat down with the investors. As my client described the situation, I could see the investors' tension rise. When he finished, the youngest of the investor group made a sweeping "no" statement. He said an additional investment was a "non-starter." The term "non-starter" is a firm way of saying "no" often made by someone in a power position, which the investors held. My client started accusing them of reneging on promises to be there when he needed them, and the situation escalated into a yelling match. Insults were exchanged, and personal attacks flew across the table in both directions.

I asked for a "time out." I took my client to another room and said, "I don't think they have really absorbed the information that you need the money for growth, and you may run out of money without an infusion, and then they may lose their original investment. Let me try to get them talking and find out why an additional investment is a 'non-starter'."

When we reentered the room and sat down, I apologized. I said to the investors that we should not have surprised you like this. I went on and explained that my client was a little surprised that the matter could not even be discussed. I said that all we want to know is why our request is a "non-starter." With a calmer environment, the investors explained that they had just had a meeting with their Board and had told them that this particular company investment was doing well. The investors' concern was with how they would explain so shortly after that reassuring meeting that they needed to invest more money in the company.

Now I was able to explain that the company was doing well but couldn't finance the growth it was facing. The problem was that the accounts receivable were growing, which was essentially loans to customers, but this created a need for cash. The investors said, "Well, OK, that is interesting. Maybe we could back an accounts receivable loan to your company secured by new purchase orders." And that is exactly what happened. The investors did not have to infuse new equity per se, but they provided a guaranty to an accounts receivable loan that financed my client's growth.

The situation was not a "non-starter." They could explain this to their Board, and everyone would be reassured and able to get what they wanted. This is a perfect pivot-from-"no" example, but it never would have happened without finding a way to better understand what was behind the "no." An additional technique was needed, borrowed from parent-child negotiations. Taking a "time out" when the situation has deteriorated to the point where parties can't listen to each other is an effective solution. When emotions are running high and parties resort to yelling and name-calling, everyone needs a "time out" to calm down and collect themselves. In our negotiation, when we reconvened and calmly explained the situation, the investors were also calmer and able to listen and find a mutually satisfying solution.

Takeaway

Unlearn the fear of "no." We need to unlearn our fear of "no," but not ignore it either. "No" can be the beginning of a great negotiation or sale. There are some who use the book *Green Eggs and Ham* as an example of persistence. In the end, Sam-I-Am sold a seemingly strange and hard-to-sell product by not giving up and basically wearing down his counterparty. This was a strategy pursued by those who sold life insurance door to door. The theory was to get inside and just wear them down until they bought insurance to get you to leave. But this is a costly solution, since it usually precludes an ongoing relationship.

Pivot off "no." As a lesson in listening, this book is a perfect example of what not to do. The questions asked by Sam-I-Am are classical closed-end probes. They create tension and such repeated backing of your counterparty into a corner, so that even if successful for this sale, it puts you in a bad spot regarding any future relationship. "No" needs to lead to questions that help you discover what exactly the objection is. You need to begin with open probes and get your counterparty talking and thinking. Get good at pivoting off "no" and you, too, can sell green eggs and ham. It may not even take you 50 words, because you should be asking, listening more, and talking less.

CHAPTER 10

LISTENING FOR RHYTHM

"Most people do not listen with the intent to understand;
they listen with the intent to reply."
—Stephen R. Covey

The Rhythm in Listening

A lot of time is devoted to teaching content in sales and negotiation settings. I went through what was referred to as the Professional Selling System when I was at Union Pacific Railroad in the mid-'80s. This approach emphasized a "needs-based" selling strategy which is designed to shift the focus from the product or service to the interests and needs of the customer. And as a lawyer, I have been to many negotiation seminars based on the book *Getting to Yes*[1] which was developed by the Harvard Negotiation Project and outlines a method for mutually successful conflict resolution.

These are excellent programs, but based on my 36-plus years of work in the field, I think we aren't teaching and learning enough about what factors, in the end, differentiate the closers and the folks who get things done on their own terms.

Skill or Alchemy?

We sometimes refer to this intangible element as instinct, or timing, or charisma. It carries the emblem of alchemy—turning base metals into gold. It is the part of sales and negotiation that engineers and technical people sometimes find hard to understand. Some think it unteachable. But it is teachable.

Great negotiators have strong technical skills and training, but what they also do well is listen carefully and get in touch with the rhythm of the person or people on the other side. Great negotiators are in touch with the back-and-forth, like martial arts masters. They are the black belts in human exchange. Face-to-face sales and negotiations are like a dance, a fight, an operatic exchange. Points and counterpoints are made through exchanges of words, gestures, tones, expressions, and emotions.

When you are trying to achieve a state of calm, do you listen to hip-hop, heavy metal, or Bob Seger? When you are looking for energy, do you listen to Beethoven and Mozart? When you are seeking to be thoughtful and think deeply, do you listen to that "Old Time Rock and Roll"? Of course you don't. We know from our own experiences that sound and cadence have an effect on our mood, mind frame, and receptivity. If you don't believe me, go to an app that has some ocean wave sounds and see if that brings you energy and motivation. Listen to Bob Seger's "Feel Like a Number" to relax yourself. Cadence has an effect on brain waves.

The popular world got really excited about "The Mozart Effect" theory that suggested certain mental tasks were improved by listening to Mozart's music. Wouldn't it be great if listening to some Mozart selections raised your IQ? The subsequent science has not been supportive of the "Effect" since the original study was published in 1993. But there is evidence that music, rhythm, and tempo do have an effect on the brain. In the journal *Psychomusicology: Music, Mind, and Brain*[2] research by Tram Nguyen found that low arousal, negative music produced the best performance for our memory. Slow and despondent apparently gets our attention.

Nguyen had participants complete three memory tasks while they listened to four types of music: high arousal, positive music (upbeat tempo and happy), high arousal, negative music (upbeat tempo but ominous tones), low arousal, positive music (low tempo but happy chords), and finally, low arousal, negative music (low tempo and despondent chords). For an example of the latter type of music, listen to "Prelude in E minor" by Frederic Chopin. The study found that participants recalled more words with low tempo music. The study further found that recognition memory was higher with low tempo and negative music like the Chopin piece.

This interesting research finding demonstrates that certain music-induced moods and arousal patterns can increase recognition memory and word recall. So, why wouldn't these findings carry over to human speech and the rhythms available to us as we speak?

The Strategies of Speaking Rhythm

Rather than try to convince you that there is a rhythm to human exchanges, I encourage you to experiment for yourself with some of the strategies and tactics below.

Strategy #1—Change the conversation— employ high arousal to disturb or disrupt

Have a conversation with a friend or significant other. Speak in a high tempo and say something you know they will disagree with. What do you get? They will likely argue with you, picking up their own tempo in the process. Saying something fast and controversial tends to turn up the heat, raise tension, and shake things up. Want to slow things down? Drop your tempo to low arousal/low tempo and say something despondent. Say something obvious or repetitive. Try this. If someone goes silent on you, they may have advanced skills which I will describe in a moment. But in general, you can change the tempo of a face-to-face exchange simply by deciding whether to say something controversial or something obvious. How quickly you say it works as an accelerator or decelerator.

Strategy #2—Back off and slow down

Specifically in a sales or negotiation context, if you are not making progress and running into lots of objections, you are not going to advance your cause by arguing. You need to back off and slow down. Say something obvious that no one can disagree with to regain your footing. And notice that this is consistent with the technical side of need-satisfaction sales. If you are having trouble closing, you need to remind your prospects of the benefits they have already accepted. If you encounter a barrier to your persuasive progress, don't pick up the pace and push harder; slow down and repeat matters already agreed upon.

Strategy #3—Identify the rhythm

To listen well in a conversation, you can't just listen to the words and watch the body language and intonation. You need to listen for, feel, and get in sync with the rhythm. Are you in a waltz? A techno-dance? A tango? Dance not your thing? Find some art you understand that has different rhythms, such as martial arts.

Everyone sitting across the negotiating table from you has a natural rhythm they have developed. Gain an advantage by figuring out what it is. You can gain their support through mirroring their rhythm. If you want to mesh with a Texan, you are going to need to slow down. If you want to mesh with a New Yorker, you are going to have to speak more quickly.

Different cultures, geographies, rural versus city, all of these have an impact on speaking patterns.

As a martial artist, I use slow rhythms like Tai Chi and fast rhythms like Karate to describe in my mind the virtual human movement I am feeling in a sale or negotiation. For my own personal style, I really love using a Jiu Jitsu rhythm for sales because it is a gentle martial art that involves deep feeling and thinking about what someone is going to do next. You can feel them before they move. It has a wonderful flow to it.

Maybe you love music. Use the different rhythms in music to keep you in touch with others around you.

Strategy #4—Go silent

Using silence is an advanced skill. Silence is truly golden when it comes to sales and negotiation. Leonardo da Vinci once said that "Nothing strengthens authority so much as silence."

What is my best tip for handling silence if you are trying to sell or trying to get a point in negotiation? Be quiet yourself. Respond in kind. When people are silent, the next statement assumes amplified importance. Someone will eventually speak, but no one will ramble, and you are much more likely to have efficiency follow the pause. Silence does not mean nothing is happening. It means people are thinking.

Some say, although I consider it an overstatement, that whoever speaks first after the silence, loses. In our noisy world today, we have lost the gift of silence. Those who practice silence are like modern Jedi Knights, practicing a long-lost martial art. In Russian martial art we spend lots of time being quiet and relaxing so we can feel others, not ourselves.

The "Calm Art of Winning" has been perfected in Russian martial art. Also called Systema or The System, it is a form of combat that has its origins back in time with Cossack warriors. It is designed to focus on hand-to-hand engagement and weapon disarmament, and its signature is an emphasis on utilizing deeply focused Zen-like calm to capture the attacker's weapons through seemingly effortless, relaxed and continuous flowing movements. Imagine an attacker comes at you with a knife. You rigidly try to block the knife. The rigidity gives the opponent structure to take advantage of. The rigid block makes me stuck and committed to this movement, and the attacker simply picks a different spot while I work to recover from my rigidity.

Strategy #5—Lose the stress

There is one sure-fire way to lose touch with the rhythm of human exchange. That is to bring stress into the situation. If you enter an exchange feeling stressed, you will never feel the rhythm of the other people. All you will feel is yourself. You enter the negotiation thinking, "I want this car for this price." You are stressed because you want this particular car, and you only buy a car once every few years. The salesperson, the finance person, and the general manager all do this every hour, every day. Stress wears you down, and eventually you make a mistake because you are tired. That is part of the reason it is such a long process. And they work to sell something to you with every detail to wear you down. Do you want the tire warranty, extended car warranty, special coating, and monthly car washes? All these decisions stress you out, and you finally say yes to some you really don't want, or maybe no to some that actually make sense. You are tired. You are stressed.

There are a variety of ways to lose the stress, most of which involve breathing techniques. There are books, apps, seminars, and endless sources to help you with this. As a martial artist, I recommend breathing and moving. If you are in a negotiation and feeling stressed, stand up and walk a bit. Let them know that you need to do a certain number of steps a day. Let them know that you have a hard time sitting. Let them know you need to stand a certain number of times a day or your Apple watch gets angry with you. I have always found that moving helps with everything. You breathe differently than when you are sitting. Standing engages muscles and gets blood flowing again. I have heard it said that "sitting is the new smoking" when it comes to health concerns. So stop sitting and move and breathe whenever you feel tension.

Takeaway

Identify and use rhythm to your advantage. Winning negotiators respect rhythm and know how to sense it and change it up. Pay attention to the rhythm of your exchanges with other people and learn how to use rhythm to redirect and win sales and negotiations. Remember that a sword drawn, high arousal (fast tempo), upbeat style is not going to bring out the best in your counterparty's ability to hear you. Slow down, relax, and make deep and meaningful points to bring out the best in the attention of the other party.

Remove the stress. If you enter a sale or negotiation in a state of stress, you will be distracted, and your focus will shift from your prospect to yourself, making it difficult, if not impossible to listen and to mirror their rhythm. When you are unable to truly listen, your potential for a successful negotiation or sale is greatly reduced. When your rhythms are not in sync, communications are not at their optimal level.

CHAPTER 11

THE IMPORTANCE OF BEING HUMAN AND HUMOROUS

"I only wish I could find an institute that teaches people how to listen. Business people need to listen at least as much as they need to talk. Too many people fail to realize that real communication goes in both directions."

—Lee Iacocca,
Former CEO Chrysler Corporation

An Introduction to Being Human

All negotiations, no matter how big or how small, are performed by humans—at least for now. Transactions, disputes, hostage crises, and all negotiation scenarios bring with them the human element and inevitable emotions. Separate the people from the problem, you say? Good luck with that. The people are the problem, and the people are the opportunity for attaining an edge.

The stronger you enter the conference room, the more superhuman you try to be, the more you try to show how smart you are, the less likely it is that I, and other counter-parties, are going to identify with you. If I don't identify with you, the odds that I will trust you go way down. So, how can I gain your trust? I need to show you exactly the opposite human characteristics. I don't need to show you I am better than you by showing how skilled and smart I am. I need to show you that I am the same as you. Trust appears when fear disappears. I need to show you I am human. This trust is more likely to develop if I approach you "softly."

"Soft v Hard Arts": Entering the Dojo

Martial artists who study more than one art often distinguish between the "hard" and "soft" martial arts. While not every-one may distinguish the two in exactly the same way, my fellow martial artists who study more than one art often dis-tinguish them by how they deal with force. A punch comes at you. You strike back hard with a block and counter punch. This describes many arts you see in traditional martial arts cinema. This describes the reaction of arts like most styles of Karate and Kung Fu. You train a technique over and over again so that when confronted with a punch, you rely on the training to "take over," and you block and return the force with a kick or punch without needing to reflect.

In a soft martial art, you focus more on breathing, moving, and instead of returning the force, you absorb or redirect. In Brazilian Jiu Jitsu, which is mostly a ground-based art, you literally roll with the punches. The same can be said of Systema, the Russian martial art. Aikido and Iaido are also soft martial arts. I studied the martial art of Iaido in Japan. It is the martial art of the Samurai. It is the art of the drawing of and the cutting with a sword. The students and teachers of Iaido are so "soft" in their art. As with most martial arts, you enter the dojo with great dignity and respect. Your walk is intentional, mindful, and relaxed. Which side you use to walk into the dojo is intentional. How you are faced as you enter the dojo is intentional. Even if there is no leader sitting at the place of honor, you act as if there is and take care when you bow so you would not have your back to the dignitary or teacher. You bow multiple times. You engage in a respectful and repetitive routine. You are reminded with each move that it is not about you. You become aware of your humility. The martial art of Iaido is about the teacher, about the dojo, and about the sword. It is not about you. You leave your ego behind.

You should enter the conference room with the same mental routine. Leave your ego behind. Enter the room prepared to learn. Enter the room with respect for the counterparty. Open your mind and your heart so you can see matters from their perspective. Enter being a human, one who is humane and prepared to understand. No path to understanding starts with sword waving. No path to understanding begins with threats. No path to understanding begins with force. My teachers and fellow students are so kind and soft and respect-ful, you would never know they are trained killers.

The Beginning of Trust: Show You Are Human

What does it mean to be human? You well may ask, "Human as opposed to what? A robot or another animal?" Some of the traits I think of when comparing robots and other animals include emotions, human errors, lying, storytelling, apolo-gizing, creativity, forgiveness, and imagination. When we perform or exhibit these traits, we appear human to others. I am not encouraging lying, but that is something we humans do. And telling a lie and then apologizing is one of the most human things we witness. Robots don't do that. Animals don't do that. People who are perfect don't do that. But ordinary humans do. Making mistakes, apologizing, and correcting them is another extremely human sequence. These human traits and sequences lead to trust. Acting perfect does not.

Making a mistake and then sincerely apologizing is one of the most powerful things for a human to do. Some of my friends like to say, "humans are the last analogue device." I was CEO of the airfreight division of the UP railroad, and we had screwed up a shipment for a major company. They were furious as we had shut down their assembly line. We were summoned to New York City. We entered the conference room ready to find out what they wanted in return. I knew it was going to be more of a spanking than a negotiation. The procurement chief, a decorated Air Force veteran, entered the room. He looked around to his staff and mine, ready to give all a lesson on how to destroy a supplier and demand recompense. Before he could begin, I said, "Sir, I want you to know that I am ashamed of our performance. It is horrible. You need to be doing business with better companies. This was awful. We were awful. On behalf of our organization, I am sorry. We are prepared to do whatever it takes to make it right. You deserve a better supplier."

I could tell he was surprised at this very honest, non-defensive, and sincere human reaction and apology. What he said next surprised even me: "Son, thank you, but I checked with our people, and this is the first issue we have had with your company. Let's figure out how to move forward. I can tell you take this seriously and it won't happen again." Imagine how it might have gone if I had not gotten the self-deprecating apology out on the table first.

Accusations and Recovery in Negotiation

I was in a heated negotiation recently. I finally caught the other side lying. I caught them dead-to-rights lying. Feeling righteous, I couldn't resist pointing that out to everyone. Did that help me progress the negotiation? Absolutely not. What happened instead was that the entire dialogue shut down because I had accused someone of dishonesty. But hey, I was right. They were being dishonest. What did I win? Nothing.

So, I immediately apologized, retracted what I said, and offered that I had misspoken. Through that conduct, I started a path back to the type of trust necessary to reach human agreements. Never, ever be afraid to apologize. Never, ever be afraid to say you were wrong—even if you were right. If your objective is to be smart and right, you will not succeed except in your own mind. In negotiations, trapping your counterparty in a corner leads to shaming or hostility. Accusations have no place when your objective is to find a solution.

Breaking the Ice in Negotiations

I can't recall a negotiation that started with entering a room or starting a call and just saying this: "We have five matters to negotiate. First, we need to agree on the split in profits; second, we need to agree on the management structure; and third, we need to agree how much we will each contribute to the venture." Never, ever, and I am speaking of 36 years of thousands of meetings between people trying to get this or that from each other. It doesn't mean that eventually those goals are not articulated; it just means that the process doesn't start that way. If negotiations don't start with negotiation goals, how do they start? Someone initiates some form of small talk. "How are you today?" "Where are you from?" "Where are you staying?" We do this because we recognize that negotiation is an inherently basic human process.

Once I was negotiating a new contract with a major manufacturing company in Idaho, and on the first visit the customer took complete control of the meeting and said, "Before we get started, here at Company A, we begin every meeting with a safety message. Today's safety message is that there is an emergency plan on the back side of your hotel room door. It shows you how and where to evacuate the hotel." And that is how it began. But even after that, we all said, "How are you doing, and where are you from?" In certain areas of the country, I have noticed, especially the South, you will not be trusted and there will not be dialogue until you exchange some personal stories.

When I was a young lawyer in Chicago at our very large law firm, I noticed we had food at every meeting. Someone in a high position of authority, knowing I was trained in business and had experience, asked me how they could make their meetings more productive. I said, "Lose the food." He looked at me like I was crazy and said, "We could never do that." I realized it was part of their culture and was not going to change, so I retracted and said the meetings were perfect as they were then.

Having food at meetings was such an embedded part of the culture that he shared my feedback with some others. Later they actually confronted me with it, saying, "I heard you thought we shouldn't have food at our meetings." It was clear that their feelings were strong about this tradition. I had to start bringing bagels myself to get back into everyone's good graces. The story is a reminder that meetings and negotiations are culturally rich exchanges. Trying to change the culture can have negative consequences.

Small talk is critical, and humor can play a role in breaking the ice as well. But don't come with a canned joke. That is what a robot would do. You need to have several in your repertoire and wait for the right moment to use them. It is best if you have something about their location and their culture to share, because that shows you care enough to learn about them. What is more human than that?

I was negotiating to invest in a community bank. I had met with the CEO of the bank and was meeting for the first time with the CFO. We were talking about negotiations generally, and I was sharing my negotiating concept of "I'm fine." The basic principle of "I'm fine" negotiating is always maneuvering the other person to make the hard decision. It is based on my description above of the soft martial arts. If you are feeling a tension in your gut due to the stress of making a decision or because you are forced into a corner, you need to find a way for the other side to make the hard decision. Like in a martial arts exchange, you are taking a punch, and you need to move and breathe and pass the tension back to the other side. I spent a couple of hours with the bank CEO and CFO, and near the end, we got to the heart of the numbers and valuation. The valuation seemed high to me. My accountant showed up near the end of the meeting. As we summarized, the CFO correctly said about me, "He thinks the value is too high." I said, "Yes, I do." It was quiet, and then the CEO looked at me and said, "Cash, I'm fine." It was a brilliant and humorous thing to say. We all laughed, and the meeting ended on a high note.

I was so impressed with the CEO because in that one phrase he showed me he had listened and understood everything I said. He got my approach and used it to show me two key things: that he was listening, and willing to negotiate with me in a way I taught and respected. To me, this was just brilliant. His star went way up in my book, and my odds of investing rose.

Human Haggling and Halfsies...

Imagine a room with two people and nothing else but a simple folding table with a candy bar sitting in the center. Eventually, one of the individuals, if not both, will want the candy bar. But something inside us human beings dictates that one person can't have it. It must be shared. Sharing is the most basic of soft skill interactions. While some people are better at it than others, we all believe fairness requires it.

A participant may try to justify something other than splitting it in half. Perhaps one will say they are hungrier, or they are bigger, or they are more deserving, or they are more needy. You can make numerous possible arguments for getting more or less than half. But the natural and implicit answer is simply to split it in half. Half is presumed fair. Sharing equally requires no argument. This moral feeling is as real as the candy bar itself. The feeling of fairness sits inside the problem and, in a metaphysical way, is present in the room. Relief comes with the outcome of sharing equally. There is then no stress. It is that fundamental.

The same is true when we negotiate. Regardless of almost any other factor, splitting the difference, what we used to call "halfsies," is considered fair. As a result, as simplistic and dumb as it sounds, there is always an implicit deal halfway between two positions. This is related to the principle behind high and low "anchors." Anchoring is a term used to describe someone putting out an initial offer that is high or low and designed to influence the midpoint. The attempted use of an anchor reinforces the theory behind halfsies. Sales are this way as well. A retailer tells you the sale price is 50% off. Fifty percent from what? A price originally set by the retailer.

There are two reasons this notion of halfsies is so important. First, it can become a benchmark for you in terms of your definition of negotiation success. The midpoint between two reasonable positions can be a guidepost for how well you do as a negotiator. Second, it should influence what you counter in your negotiation. Suppose you are buying a car that has a sticker of $45,000. You have done your research and found that this car has a range of values and that deals have been done, at the low end, for as little as $39,000. You push the dealer for their best price, and she shows you the invoice is $43,000. So now you have a range of reasonable prices from $39,000 to $43,000, and arguably, anything in that range is a reasonable outcome. Halfsies will tell you there is an implied deal at the midpoint of $41,000. But if in your next move you split the difference and go halfsies at $41,000, the dealer will drive the new result to $42,000 which is the new midpoint. In fact, a savvy dealer will counter you at $42,500 allowing you to think you do well when she accepts your counteroffer at $42,000. You need to plan your offers to maintain the original midpoint.

Halfsies generally works when you are already in a range of reasonableness. When parties are very far apart, the principle of halfsies can work just like a third-party confirmation or an external fact like "market price." Suppose you want to buy a house and the asking price is $500,000. You offer $450,000 because you think that $475,000 is a reasonable price. On the next move the seller comes down only $5,000 to $495,000. That move is designed to send a message to you that the deal will not settle at $475,000. The message is, "no" to a halfsies process. The seller is using the principle of halfsies to message you about where the endpoint will be.

Takeaway

Walk into a room like a superpower and master of the universe, and you lose power. That entry may massage your ego but will not help you or your client if you are representing someone else. Find your human side to deal with other humans. Show your weaknesses, point out your mistakes, bring yourself down a level. Be humble. Now the counterparties like you. Now they trust you. Because just like them, you are a flawed human being out there doing your best. They may even want to help you and will surely want to deal with you again.

Make sure you understand the innately human and nearly genetic sense of fairness. If you pay attention to feelings of fairness, like halfsies, you will be able to complete transactions in a way consistent with these fundamental and deeply rooted human elements.

CHAPTER 12

SPEAKING—SAY THIS, NOT THAT

Words do two major things: They provide food for the mind
and create light for understanding and awareness.

—Jim Rohn

When Choices Grow Up

I grew up in Upstate New York, and virtually all my friends were of Italian descent. Back then, only my Italian friends' families used olive oil, so I got to taste it plain, drizzled on fresh, crunchy bread, poured lightly over pizza, and stirred carefully into thick, rich pasta sauces. This was quite a departure from my own Welsh, Franco-German, Slavic family kitchen with its roots deep in dairy farming. We used butter for everything. And when butter wasn't the right accompaniment to a dish, there was mayonnaise whipped up from fresh farm eggs.

Back then, I didn't know that I was eating artery-clogging meals or that my friends were eating meals that would keep them healthy and living a longer life. Today, things are different. There are dozens of books, websites, podcasts, and countless studies and journal articles that teach us to "eat this, not that" to get and stay healthy. We now know to eat lean turkey instead of mayonnaise-loaded tuna salad. We know to use olive oil instead of butter or margarine. We have learned to substitute less-healthy foods with healthier ones.

Our choices have grown up, just as we have. Our knowledge and understanding about the consequences of our choices have also grown. Now the challenge before us is to take action on the better choices we know about.

Substitution is an Easier Form of Change

Substituting a healthier food for a similar but less-healthy one will bring a more advantageous outcome and is easier than dieting. Why is this easier? Because you aren't stopping your behavior. You don't have to stop eating a food entirely. You are simply eating something different. In the grocery store, the kitchen, and in restaurants, you are just trading one food for another that will bring a better overall outcome. "Eat this, not that" becomes the strategy for dietary change at the dining table.

The same substitution strategy works at the negotiating table. Bad listening habits that lead to unsatisfactory outcomes, like bad eating habits, are also more easily corrected with substitutions. "Say this, not that" becomes an excellent strategy for change at the negotiating table. You can learn to substitute language elements and usage that will bring better results during negotiations.

The Core Elements of Language Substitution

Talking and listening are basic, rudimentary life skills and essential elements of the human interactive process. They can lead to effective communication, which is the basis of getting things done together, or they can lead to a breakdown in communication and result in a failed cooperative effort and negotiation. Language substitution can also lead to uncovering "back stories" to help you understand what someone wants.

Communication is a foundation of any negotiation process. Language is the means by which we express our positions and seek to understand the position of the counterparty. The extent to which participants communicate efficiently and effectively will often determine the outcomes.

Many responsive phrases can be "showstoppers" and impose impediments to the progress of communication. Showstopping phrases tend to introduce emotion into communication and evoke ego reactions. By avoiding these phrases and substituting others using the "Say this, not that" approach, you have a simple and effective way to accelerate progress in communicating and a better chance for accomplishing cooperative negotiations.

Showstoppers in a martial arts or physical setting are like fighting words. You say the wrong thing, and you incite a fight. You give a "hard look," i.e., a confrontational stare, you get the same back. You say, "F you," and you get "F you" back. If you get in a confrontational or aggressive stance, fight or flight human genes kick in to get you ready for a battle. Fight or flight leads to short, quick breaths, more rapid heartbeat, and other "get ready for a fight" physical reactions. These physical reactions can likewise be incited by words and phrases.

In a confrontational setting, especially one where the parties are focused on winning, we all introduce phrases that aren't constructive but make us feel better, both knowingly and unknowingly, and often unintentionally. Not only are many of these phrases not constructive, but they are destructive. They lead to breakdowns in communication, block listening, create walls instead of doors, and disrupt the communication and negotiation process. These are phrases that halt the conversation. They are showstoppers.

Avoid the showstoppers unless you are trying to evoke tension. Before you speak, consider whether your choice of words is constructive or destructive. It is possible you want to introduce disruption into the negotiation. Maybe it isn't going the way you had hoped. Maybe you don't think the other side is being honest with you, and you want to ramp up the tension to bring out their true intentions. These phrases or verbal tactics can feel similar to someone walking out of the room.

I was negotiating a second round of financing for a company I had founded. The company was not doing well and needed more capital than any of us had thought it would. The economy had collapsed, and there were a few surprises in the business. Early on, as we were describing the challenges that caused us to request more capital, one of the younger partners said, "Let me tell you again why it isn't going to happen; I don't think you get it." That statement lit me and my team up, and we got emotional and angry. I now recognize that the senior partners had planned this to see just where we were. They knew we would be choosing our words carefully, and we would be well-scripted, which we were. But one showstopper phrase and, like an amateur fighter thrown off balance by an unexpected punch, the careful planning on our side went right out the window. Suddenly the terms of our refinancing got worse. We walked right into a disruptive communication tactic and responded defensively.

So, whether you want to disrupt or calm things down, consider some of the following phrases and consider their substitutes: "Say this, not that."

1. Say "I understand," not "Calm down."

When conversations get heated, and you are listening to someone rant and rave, you may be tempted to say "Relax" or "Calm down" in an attempt to cool the boiling waters. This never works. In fact, it tends to amplify already angry emotions. The speaker takes your attempts to bring the temperature down as criticism. A better alternative is to say nothing, let them run their course, and when they are finished, simply say "I understand." This results in a dialogue that can go on from that point in a productive way, with both sides discussing issues and working toward a positive outcome. If you are seeking a skirmish, looking to raise the volume, or trying to uncover true intention, go ahead and tell them to calm down.

2. Say "Let me try explaining again," not "You don't get it," or "You aren't listening."

This phrasing "You don't get it" is more common in tech circles. When I was in the Bay Area in the '90s there were two kinds of people, if you used the nomenclature of the day. There were the "They don't get it" people, which meant, for example, that they didn't understand that revenue didn't matter when it came to dot coms. In that day, dot coms were exempt from accepted, traditional laws of finance and business. "They don't get it" is combative. It is an insult. It creates a "them and us" divisive scenario which is not conducive to listening or effective cooperative negotiation. A much better substitute if you want to get progress is to say "I did a bad job of explaining my point. Let me try again."

3. Say "Great idea," not "That's what I said."

In discussions, the other party may hijack an idea you had and present it as their own. The temptation is to grab the credit by responding with the phrase, "That's what I said." However true that might be, pointing out that it was your idea and you had already said it is mostly your ego at work.

You are seeking to show someone you are smarter than they are. You are simply looking to claim rights to that original thought, idea, or concept. After all, if you had it first, then you are smarter than the counterparty. This immediately creates a competitive, even combative atmosphere which is counter-productive to effective negotiation. Try switching to a less-charged and ego-centric phrase like, "I agree" or "Great idea." This simple substitution has the power to defuse the situation and get the conversation back on track.

4. Say "Let me put it another way," not "You're not listening!"

If you are in a conversation with someone and you don't think they are listening, I guarantee you they will hear one statement very well: "You aren't listening." It is a criticism of them. Using any statement or choice of words that is explicitly or implicitly critical will get in the way of communication progress. If you don't feel the other side is getting your point, try, "Let me put this another way." However, if you are trying to be disruptive, uncover backstory, or shake things up, "You aren't listening" will get you a reaction.

5. Say "I was thinking," not "Actually."

This is a personal pet peeve of mine. When you are listening to someone and then you say, "Actually," you are in fact correcting them by sounding superior. It is an insult served up with a giant scoop of ego on top. How about substituting "I was thinking" or "I was wondering," two phrases that give you the same result without the overlay of insult, ego, and superiority. So, if you are seeking to disrupt, say "Actually" as often as you can.

6. Say "What should we do about that," not "I know."

If you do know, that's good. But keep it to yourself if you want to make forward progress in communication. "I know" is the opposite of "Actually" and is defensive in nature. To make progress in a negotiation, substitute a phrase like "What should we do about that?" It is a better choice for keeping negotiations proceeding when you are tempted to say, "I know."

7. Say "I agree," or "That makes sense," not "Of course."

When you say "Of course," it sends a signal to the other speaker that you think they are stating the obvious. The result often is to make them feel stupid. The phrase, "Of course" introduces ego and one-upmanship. A better phrase is simply to say ,"I agree," which reinforces and advances negotiating points.

Takeaway

"Say this, not that" phrases are designed to reduce ego assertion and tension in communication and negotiation.

As a listener, you will help negotiations progress to a more positive outcome by avoiding phrases and words that cause shields to go up and provoke other parties to become angry or defensive. Resolution, and, ultimately, your progress in a negotiation, will be based in large part not only on how well you listen, but on the words you choose for responding to what you hear. If you seek progress, then choose the words that will help lower shields and open possibilities.

If you desire to disrupt the process in order to uncover motives or positions that aren't clear, then just "Say that, not this" and reverse the strategy. But remember, if you decide to disrupt, be prepared for the consequences. Refer to a subsequent chapter in this book, "The Value of Unreasonable People," and get ready for some counterpunching that may well go beyond what you intended.

How well you respond when you are listening and learning to use strategic phrases is not only critical to a satisfactory negotiation outcome, but it is also critical to your career advancement. Use "Say this, not that" choices that make communication and negotiation more efficient and effective. Use "Say that, not this" choices to make the process more tense or difficult if you can handle the consequences and it serves your goals.

CHAPTER 13

THE HONESTY STRATEGY

Who speaks, sows; who listens, reaps.
—Argentine Proverb

The Emperor's New Clothes

My favorite fable as a child was Hans Christian Andersen's
"The Emperor's New Clothes."[1] Even though it was published
in 1837, almost 200 years ago, it still has a valuable lesson to
teach us today. It can teach much about today's workplace,
most importantly about the power of honesty.

Two swindlers come to a town where there lives a vain
emperor who loves to dress in fashionable clothes. They
convince the emperor to let them sew him a suit of clothes
that will be the envy of all other rulers. He pays them the
outlandish fee they demand, and they order the expensive
fabrics and gold and silver trim to make the emperor's new

clothes. However, instead of ordering the lavish materials, they pocket the fee and set to work sewing a set of invisible clothes. To make sure that no one exposes their scam, they announce that the clothes are special. They are invisible to anyone unfit to do their job.

While they are busy in their workplace sewing the clothes, the emperor sends some of his most trusted counselors to inspect the progress. Not one of the counselors can see the clothes. But, fearful of being seen as inept and losing their lofty positions at court, each counselor extolls the beauty and artistry of the new clothes. Reassured by his counselors, the emperor decides to show off his new clothes once they are finished by parading through the town wearing them, so that everyone can admire him.

He sets off proudly wearing the invisible clothes. Everyone cheers as he passes. Everyone marvels at the fine new clothes the emperor is wearing. Everyone except a young boy who watches the emperor pass by and shouts, "Hey, the emperor has no clothes!"

And that's the story of the vain emperor who paraded through his town stark naked until one honest boy shouted the truth for all to hear.

The Danger of Collective Self-Deception

What is the moral of the story, and how does it apply to today's workplace and negotiations? To me, the moral of the story is about the dangers of "group think" and the decisions that can result from this kind of herd mentality. This is especially counter-productive in negotiating situations. It illustrates how a group collectively can make a bad decision that a single individual would not. Everyone in the fable knows the emperor is not wearing any clothes, but they are afraid to say anything because they think others will perceive them as unfit for their jobs.

If you want to be a great contributor to a great organization as well as a great negotiator, you need to watch out for both personal self-deception and collective self-deception caused by "group think." As my good friend and mentor Cathy B. Colella—a former Ford model and CEO of an environmental remediation company—used to warn me: "When you hear this dishonesty driven by a fear of not agreeing, you have to be the child in the room and fearlessly and honesty point out that 'the emperor has no clothes.'"

How can you identify these "group think" situations? There are several clues that you can watch for, certain phrases, tones, and behaviors to help you spot group self-deception, denial, and bad decision-making in the works. Here are some examples of what it sounds like in meetings, in company emails, and in simple conversations or complex negotiations.

Verbal Clues

The following are some phrases associated with self-denial and bad decision-making I have heard over the years, which came up in projects I led or participated in—projects that didn't have a good outcome. These projects would have had much better results had I engaged in the transactions with brutal honesty and straight dialogue.

#1—"It's strategic."

This can often mean that in the financial calculations the numbers themselves don't make sense. Using the word "strategic" is designed to hide this fact behind the concept of strategic planning rather than staying focused on sound financial decision-making.

#2—"They don't get it."

This is a dismissive phrase signaling that you if you don't agree, you are stupid or at least unenlightened. It is designed to cut off dialogue and debate.

#3—"Don't worry about it. That isn't your concern."

Generally, this means you should worry about it. If you uncover something the organization needs to know about, and you are deeply concerned about it, yet someone says this to you, it's important to find a way to raise the issues with those who would worry about it, those higher in the chain of command.

#4—Any *ad hominem* attacks

These are attacks on individuals instead of their arguments and sound something like this: "Joe is an idiot and doesn't have a clue." If you hear this type of phraseology, you should consider it a red flag that this topic or a part of the negotiation needs further debate and discussion. This personal attack strategy is often used to divert attention away from significant issues or cogent arguments.

#5—Changing the subject

Some people are masterful at changing the subject. In workplace discussions, meetings, and negotiations, you may sometimes reach a difficult place in the dialogue or analysis. Then, all of a sudden, someone changes the subject. Your response should be to bring the discussion back to the main topic as quickly as you can.

#6—Evaluating seemingly insignificant distinctions

Sometimes you will be in a meeting or sitting at the negotiating table and find a problem with a proposed course of action or suggested plan. You may see an apparently small deviation from an expected trajectory in certain outcomes presented. Listen carefully and consider whether the distinctions matter. If they do, bring them to the attention of your team or team leader. If they don't, then table them for discussion at a later time. I was once working on an acquisition early in my career when I noticed that the growth rate for the target company seemed too high. When our team questioned it, the deal champion said that this was a slightly different segment and would grow faster. However, it didn't follow the projected course. In that case, the seemingly insignificant distinctions made a significant difference.

#7—Twisting the facts to make them fit the decision

In some situations, everyone agrees on the facts, but negotiations still reach an impasse. When this happens, pay very close attention during later meetings to see if someone tries to rewrite the facts to get past the impasse. We were negotiating an acquisition when I was a young lawyer. The industry growth rates were not fast enough to justify the price the seller wanted. Our Executive VP, who really wanted the deal, defined a new industry segment in a way that was growing fast enough to justify the price. In the end, we grossly overpaid for the acquisition.

#8—One-sided overselling

If a proposed decision or course of action is overly presented through exaggerated tones or hyperbole, or if only the positives are presented, you should take this as a clue to dig deeper. A good presentation of a proposed decision should have a balanced view. Both positives and negatives should be represented.

#9—Use of brute force or politics

Listen for language, especially tones that signal desperation. For example, "We must do this deal, or they will disband our deal team." These are cues that should make your negotiating antenna quiver. Politics is the use of indirect means to get approvals that wouldn't be granted if the proper issues were considered in an atmosphere free of pressure or undue influence. People with a stake in the outcome will push you to make a deal that may not be sound. An investor who wants a better return on their investment will encourage you to take on more acquisitions and more debt, even though it may dramatically increase your risk.

#10—"It's synergistic or 1 + 1 = 3."

This formula comes up in the context of acquisitions, mergers, and combinations. It's not that such a synergistic scenario isn't conceptually possible; however, it generally takes longer and requires more work to move it to a successful completion. Acquisitions are often price justified based on the fact that costs can be cut because the firms can share overhead. But the process of that implementation can be more challenging than it appears "pre-deal." And there is always a possibility that successful completion will never happen.

Own the Power of Honesty

You may think you don't have the power or that you are taking a huge risk when you raise a red flag in response to behaviors and language designed to prevent open and honest discussion. You wouldn't be wrong in this concern. There is always a risk whenever you speak up about such things. But my advice is to take the risk. Like the little boy in the fable of the emperor and his invisible clothes, be fearless in pointing out the truth. It's the truth that matters. Truth and honesty will bring about debate that furthers better decision-making.

From a martial arts perspective, one has to be very honest about where you are in your abilities and avoid self-deception about the difference between training in a dojo and the real world. In the dojo, you train with people who have similar training. Your training partner tells you what strike they will do so you practice blocking. Your training partner will move slowly and deliberately. You get the feeling of confidence in the dojo. But outside the dojo, risks come at you randomly. You don't take off your shoes before conflict. It just happens. Those training in martial arts often go through a phase I have referred to as "the tiger phase." The student wants to engage to show what she or he knows. But there is a big difference between feeling ready for conflict and being ready for a fight. I remember my mentor Cathy B. Colella saying to me, "You have fire in your belly, but you need to have blood in your mouth." I know that sounds strange, but what she was telling me was that I needed to have stronger execution in my current conflict, and not just a bold, tough attitude. Be honest with yourself about where you are.

Takeaway

An effective approach is to provide input to your organization with childlike innocence, not know-it-all aggression. If your organization doesn't want to hear your innocent questions when you speak up and point out behaviors that hinder sound organizational decision-making, then you may need a new organization. Great companies and great leaders welcome robust and honest debate and seek the input of all.

Listen, listen, listen for voice tones, phrases, and words that are designed to derail good decision-making processes. Watch for disruptive and obstructive behaviors. Having said that, if your organization, after carefully listening to all the input, decides to go a certain direction and you disagree, it is time for you to support the organizational decision. This is essential to ensure corporate functionality and discipline.

As Peter Nulty wrote in *Fortune* magazine, "Of all the skills of leadership, listening is the most valuable—and one of the least understood. Most captains of industry listen only sometimes, and they remain ordinary leaders. But a few, the great ones, never stop listening. That's how they get word before anyone else of unseen problems and opportunities."[2]

CHAPTER 14

BACKSTORIES AND HOW TO UNCOVER WHAT IS REALLY GOING ON

> *"There are more things in heaven and earth, Horatio,*
> *than are dreamt of in your philosophy."*
> —Hamlet, I.5

"That Doesn't Make any Sense"

The above phrase is one of the most common phrases in negotiations, both said to the counterparty and said internally within a negotiating team about some position the counterparty is taking. After all the years I have spent negotiating and being part of negotiating teams, I have come to understand that most of the time if something doesn't make sense, it is not because we are stupid and they are crazy (although that can be true, it is rare). If something doesn't make sense, I assume there is something I don't know. There are facts not known to me that make their position look unreasonable or obscure. Instead of fighting with them over that position, it means I have to find those facts that would make their position rational and understandable. I need to find the backstory. And there is almost always a backstory. To find the backstory, like Hamlet, we have to accept there are things we don't know and expand our observational skills. This means not being confined by logic we learn at the university.

In one of my first deals, I was the junior associate at a major law firm, and we were representing a major commodities company. Our client was buying the U.S. assets of a major international brewing company. We didn't know much about the company, and neither did the clients. All our clients knew was they could buy these assets at a pretty good price. The international company selling the assets was in a big hurry, so we traveled to the Midwestern city where the U.S. division was headquartered. I recall the seller being pushy and anxious. They were willing to sell at a good price if our client moved quickly. This, of course, made us (the lawyers and the clients) nervous. We spent a lot of time on representations and warranties which are protections in case there was something we didn't know that later came back to haunt us, like an undisclosed liability.

We were meeting in a large conference room at the target's headquarters. Someone asked me if they could get me coffee. I wasn't raised with people waiting on me, and if anything,

I was used to getting things for others. So I said, "Thanks, I will be happy to get it; just point me in the right direction." I even asked if anyone else wanted anything. A couple of others said they wanted coffee. Hey, I was the junior associate, so it made sense. As I entered the kitchen, I looked around. It was well outfitted. It was more like a Four Seasons than an office kitchen. The silverware, the mugs, napkins, plates, tables, and cupboards were high end. I found the coffee maker and made coffee. I looked in the refrigerator, and it was full of beer. I was surprised. There was other alcohol in the cupboards.

That night at dinner, I told the partner above me and the client what I had seen and found. The president of the commodities company said it was very interesting and complimented me on my observational skills. Nothing further was said. In day two of the negotiation, I noticed that our client, led by the president, was slowing the negotiation. He had clearly changed his approach compared to the day before. The next night at dinner, the president said in front of everyone, "Cash, it may not be something they teach you in law school, but that little observation really helped us." As it turns out, the president, using my observation as a lead, checked around the industry and found out the two executives that the foreign company had sent to the U.S. to run the division had partied nonstop and, among other things, had put losing trading positions in place. The upshot of it was the target company was bleeding cash. This was an extremely desperate sale, and that was the rush. We shaved another $5 million off the sale, and whether I deserved it or not, I got a significant amount of the credit for this, due to my paying attention and finding the backstory. The backstory was that a couple of Aussies who had never been to the U.S. were having the time of their lives and had destroyed the U.S. operation. The evidence was throughout the kitchen, and I had seen it.

Finding the Backstory: Think Like Colombo and Ask Questions Like an Investigative Reporter

Colombo was my favorite TV show as a kid. This unassuming detective who wore an old raincoat had several important skills. He asked simple questions and didn't stop until he had an answer. If he didn't understand the answer or doubted the veracity of the answer, he tried asking again another way. He was a persistent listener. He just wouldn't stop until he got an answer, and then he would actively listen and confirm it. If it was inconsistent with other information, he would point that out to the speaker and try again. He would ask if the speakers were sure and why they were sure and ask them to explain the inconsistency he had discovered. If nothing else, he wore them down.

Detective Columbo would also shadow his suspects. He would follow them everywhere. He would get to know the suspect. He would become friends with the suspect. All this time he was learning about the suspects as people, learning their habits, learning their speech. He was a sponge. Much like my experience with "the kitchen full of alcohol," he would notice anything that was out of order. He was a detail nut.

He noticed that a murder victim's shoes were tied in such a manner that they were likely tied by another person, because the laces that were on top in the knot were the laces that would be on the bottom if tied by the person themselves.

To find the backstory, you have to be like Columbo. You have to ask questions. You can't stop until you get answers that make sense. You have to question inconsistencies and doubt, or at least be skeptical of, what counterparties say. Become an obsessive observer and a lover of detail. Spend time with your counterparty either virtually or in person. You need to observe them in their "natural habitat," as Mutual of Omaha's *Wild Kingdom* TV program used to say.

An additional strategy is to test your counterparty's reaction. In martial arts, there is a lot of feigning. You pretend to throw a kick or punch, and you see the reaction. Watch any UFC (Ultimate Fighting Championship) fight or boxing match, and you will see this common tactic. What does it tell you? It tells you what to expect and what you will face if you follow through on that tactic. I was in a bar in Texas with some friends, and there was a young lady being harassed by a man I hadn't seen before. We knew the young lady; she was a regular. One of us said, "Hey, she wants you to leave her alone; could you do that?" The guy turned to confront us. I took him in and practiced listening. I looked to see if I could discern a weapon. And then I reached quickly into my pocket. As I did that, he looked down at his left boot. I discerned from that he had a weapon, probably a knife, inside his boot. We asked the young lady to join us and moved away from him.

When people have a weapon, if they feel threatened, they check to see its availability and their ease of getting to it. I concluded he was armed.

Takeaway

Watch some old episodes of *Columbo*. He may not have been a negotiator, but he always figured out who the perpetrator was with keen observational skills, investigative journalism skills, and just plain being around his "counterparty." Ask your counterparty why they want what they want, not just what they want. And then doubt the answer. They will likely try to withhold from you their real reasons, so don't take the "why" at face value. Find the "why" by becoming Columbo the detective.

Then, like Columbo, you'll uncover the backstory. Knowing that backstory will make you a more effective negotiator. The counterparty's position will make sense or at least be understandable. You can reach better decisions about whether and how to pursue your goals.

CHAPTER 15

THE POWER OF SINCERITY

> *The merit of originality is not novelty;*
> *it is sincerity.*
>
> —Thomas Carlyle

"Sincerely…"

If you want to get what you want, sincerity is essential. But what is sincerity exactly? It is a word we take for granted. It appears at the end of virtually every piece of correspondence I have ever received or sent. It has to be the most common complementary close. We say, "sincerely" throughout our correspondence. But do we actually mean it? It's worth exploring just what sincerity means to us.

Discovering sincerity

For me, when I write "Sincerely," I mean it. I know what it means because I went to church every Sunday as a child (I was not given a choice), and while I admit tuning out of many a sermon, I do remember the sermon about sincerity very well.

I spent what once was called the "Wonder Bread" years in Pittsburgh where my dad was a faculty member and head of the computer department at the school then called Carnegie Tech, now Carnegie Mellon. We lived a long way from the nearest Nazarene church, which was my mother's religion. Every Sunday, the minister, Dallas Mucci, would structure his sermons in ways as to include a fascinating historical point. He drew us in, something not easy to accomplish with a 12-year-old like me, who would rather be playing hockey in the streets or baseball in the park with friends.

On one Sunday in particular, Pastor Mucci spoke about the word "sincere," saying specifically that we needed to be sincere with God. As it turns out, that didn't mean we had to be perfect. It meant we needed to be who we were. He taught us that the word "sincere" literally meant "without wax." So, we were to approach God without wax? The etymology of the word, he explained, came from a time when artisans made pots for the king or queen. The pots they fashioned would have imperfections, maybe a bump here or there or a little air pocket. The surface wasn't perfectly smooth. If you were a pottery maven, you could sand down the bumps to smooth out the surface. But then what could you do with the tiny holes? You could fill them with wax. By adding the wax, you could present a "perfect" pot.

But actually, the pot was not perfect. Pastor Mucci said that a pot made without wax, "sincere," was the truly perfect pot. He added that sometimes pots would be ordered "sincere," made without wax.

That sermon was hard to tune out. It stayed with me. And to this day, every time I sign an email or a letter, I always use the word "sincere." I use that word because I mean what I am saying. There is "no wax" in my letters or correspondence to cover up hidden meanings. What I write is what it is. You can count on it.

"No wax" negotiations

As you negotiate, imagine the power you can exert throughout the process by having a reputation of being sincere and communicating with sincerity. One result is that you will tend to bring out the sincerity in others. Another result is that sincerity is like smiling. It's contagious. This is because, in many ways, negotiation is a tit for tat, ping-pong type of engagement. In many ways, you get what you give.

In the martial arts, to me this sincerity is exhibited and reflected in our constant bowing. We bow to the shomen (the front of the dojo) when we enter. We bow as we enter the mat. We bow to our teacher. We bow to our fellow student. We bow before we spar (practice fighting). We bow after we spar. We bow at the end of class. We bow as we leave the dojo. With each bow we are expressing humility and respect. We mean each other no harm. We are sincere in our desire to learn, not hurt, and respect the techniques and traditions that are being shared with us.

"I Yam What I Yam"

Popeye was a cartoon I loved. I never quite understood if it was a commercial for spinach, a recruiting tool for the Navy, a lesson for men on how to treat women, or a commentary on sincerity. Now, this comic strip character is over 90 years old. Today one of Popeye's most memorable quotes is the iconic "I Yam What I Yam."

To me, this iconic quote expresses that you honestly meant what you said. It means your words are "without wax." This can be a valuable asset at the negotiating table. If your counterparty accepts that you are sincere, everything you say is taken with greater confidence. This perception and belief in your sincerity is especially helpful when you near the end of a negotiation and want to stand your ground on a specific point.

The same holds true for the sign-off "Sincerely" at the end of your correspondence. When you are a person known to be sincere, then what you have expressed in your writing will be taken with greater confidence.

The Sincerity Principle in Action

Recently I was involved in a mediation where establishing sincerity helped move us toward an acceptable conclusion. One of my companies was the defendant in a quasi-class action suit. The case was set for mediation. I conveyed to the mediator and our counsel that, in the scheme of things, I considered this a 4 out of 10 in terms of priority. I explained in detail why I gave this rating and described the other matters I had to address, matters that involved great opportunities. I said that, while I was glad to participate as CEO and ultimate decision-maker, I had limited time to devote to this mediation. I made it very clear that if the mediation was not going to come to an efficient conclusion that day, I would be moving on to other things and they could deal with counsel only. It wasn't a threat. I was sincere. I was being Popeye.

Throughout that mediation, whenever I engaged with the mediator, I politely reminded him that I respected the process and wanted to give it a good chance. I also reminded him that I would be available only for a limited time, but that I was ready to commit to a specific sum. I explained that I knew it would be expensive to continue, but that ultimately, I was fairly confident, even after spending a million dollars to defend, we would likely prevail. The original demand was, let's say, for $10 million. I had every intention of potentially settling for $250,000, but only my counsel knew that.

We reached a point in the mediation after several hours where the other party was in the half-a-million range, and the mediator said he didn't think they would move any further. I authorized counsel to go as high as $269,000 and told the mediator that, indeed, it was time for me to tend to other matters. I pointed out to the mediator that I had given my best and final settlement offer to counsel and had enjoyed our working together. The mediator said, "Cash, you have been consistent and clear from the beginning, and I respect that."

The case didn't settle that day but settled only slightly higher than my number a week later. This was a situation where sincerity shone, and the mediators knew I was being honest and clear about my approach and parameters.

Takeaway

Earning a reputation for sincerity brings strength into your negotiations. Here are four key points you can take to heart in both negotiations and life:

1. Sincerity is valuable in negotiations since it is contagious and, as a result, can help bring both parties closer together.
2. Sincerity doesn't need any frills; it is simply you being your authentic self in every communication and negotiation.
3. Sign every piece of correspondence with the word "Sincerely" as a reminder that you don't need "the wax" to conceal meanings or hide anything.
4. Show respect for your counterparties with a symbolic mental bow. Not a physical bow but an internal one.

CHAPTER 16

THE VALUE OF UNREASONABLE PEOPLE

All progress depends on the unreasonable man.
—George Bernard Shaw

Some of the Best Deals Involve Unreasonable People

I consider myself a reasonable person and by that, I simply mean that I believe in logic, fair play, integrity, and sincerity in negotiations. If I agree with the counterparty that the point is resolved, I don't revisit it unless new facts emerge. Facts matter. Logic matters. I have developed a reputation for straightforward negotiations. But clients don't always share that approach, nor do other team members when teams are involved.

Some of the best deals I have done have involved unreasonable team members and clients because they push the deal and the counterparty to their limits. A recent article in *Inc. Magazine,* entitled "Why Being Unreasonable Pays Off,"[1] underscores my personal experience with unreasonableness by pointing out that in Billy Shore's book, *The Imaginations of Unreasonable Men,*[2] he talks about three philosophical underpinnings of breakthrough thinking: that good is not good enough; that most failures are failures of imagination; and that irrational self-confidence can be a good thing. "Without these three convictions," says Shore, "most efforts to solve our toughest problems will falter... Taken together," he concludes, "they affirm the wisdom of George Bernard Shaw who said, 'The reasonable man adapts himself to the world; the unreasonable one persists in trying to adapt the world to himself. Therefore all progress depends on the unreasonable man.'"

Three stories will help in understanding the value and limitations of the "Unreasonable."

Story #1—The Unreasonable Texas Utility CEO

A client of mine, a CEO of a Texas utility, had successfully taken the utility public. A few years later, a large private equity fund bought the utility, taking it private again. My client had indications that the new ownership group was planning to terminate his employment agreement. He wanted to get in front of the issue, so he contacted me, and we got to work to shift from a defensive position to an offensive position.

Tactic #1—Discombobulation and the preemptive strike. Before he even got notice of termination, he pushed for us to send the equity fund a letter initiating discussions. This step could be seen by more reasonable people as being unnecessarily preemptive. After all, the CEO hadn't yet received any formal notification that his employment was about to be terminated.

This is one of the characteristics of unreasonable people—they tend to push you to act before you otherwise would. This strategy can yield a strong strategic advantage. And that's exactly what happened in this case. The preemptive and unreasonable strike by the CEO allowed us to take control of the timing and set the tone and pace for all future communication. It was a discombobulating move.

Tactic #2—Response to a rigid "take it or leave it" offer. The owners made the CEO a defensible offer, but at a fraction of what he argued he should be getting. Negotiations proceeded, and then we reached a stalemate. To push past the stalemate, the owners took an extreme step and sent a courier with a check for a million dollars to the CEO's house with a "take it or leave it" note. I vividly remember thinking how obnoxious that was, since they did not give me any notice. I'm sure that tactic empowered and encouraged both me and my client. This emphasizes how much negotiation is a tit for tat social process. After the stalemate, my client became like Hamlet. He seemed to put on a cloak of unreasonableness.

Tactic #3—The cloak of unreasonableness. The CEO detached from me. He detached from everyone around him. He basically acted as if he were willing to blow to pieces any progress already made. I will never forget when I had to deliver the news to the opposition that everything was off the table, that there was no progress and there was no deal. I informed them that the CEO had issued a blanket rejection. He dug in his heels. It was clear and unequivocal that he would rather destroy the company than reach a deal with the new owners. He even went so far as to voice his position to some current and former employees. The new owners sitting on the other side of that negotiation and their legal counsel asked for a call with me during which they said, "Your client is crazy."

"I know," I replied. "What are we going to do?" We ultimately settled for about seven times the original offer. I honestly would have settled for less, but my client's unreasonableness and crazy disposition got us a better deal. Because of their tactic of sending the courier with the rigid "take it or leave it" offer, the counterparty opened the door to unreasonable tactics.

Story #2—The Unreasonable Partner and His Selling Price

My business partner and I were selling a company. I took on the role of the negotiator. As we began discussions, the buyer wanted to know how much we wanted for the company. Since my partner owned more of the company than I did and was significantly older, I thought he should set the price. After all, I reasoned logically, the company was his life's work. He gave me a number to include in the letter of intent. I thought the price he wanted was pretty high. So, I did my due diligence. I checked around on multiples to ensure we got a fair price.

As we moved deeper into negotiating the transaction, the buyer, as buyers do, began to raise issues designed to diminish the value of the company and decrease the price.

Tactic #1—Stand firm if unreasonable. No matter what financial offer I took to my partner, he was not dissuaded from his original asking price for the company. He stayed firm. He was persistent and unflappable. Soon, even I began to think that he was being unreasonable and illogical. His recalcitrance started to get to me. Had he been negotiating the deal, we never would have reached closure. But ultimately, his seemingly unreasonable stance got us a better deal.

Story #3—The Unreasonable Negotiator and the Developer

I was negotiating with a developer on a property adjacent to one of the buildings in which I own several condos. The developer and I established a good relationship, and we were making great progress. There was a member on my team who had lots of experience dealing with developers and developments. Doing this was her business. Now and then she would inject demands into the negotiation that were on the edge, and we managed to get them integrated.

As we approached the end of the negotiation, I had a feeling she was going to pull back. If you negotiate enough, you begin to sense the style of those around you. This sensing is similar to martial arts where you come to recognize that some opponents start strong, and some lie back and work to surprise you. I sensed she was aggressive, then would lie back, and then come on with surprises. The developer and his team sensed this underlying shift also.

Then the surprise happened. Just when we were getting ready to conclude our negotiation, the developer's team introduced a new element. They asked for a crane easement. By introducing a new element, the developer's team opened the door to a little tit for tat. My teammate sprung up and started adding several new demands as well as additional money for the easement. When I presented those new demands, it was not surprising that the counterparty was reluctant and expressed doubt that we would even be able to reach an agreement.

However, I was able to point out that it was their last-minute ask that led to new items. The unreasonable negotiator takes tactical advantage of every modification that appears as negotiations move toward a final deal. We worked through it and reached what we all believed was a mutually beneficial deal. This was a recent deal, and I consider it a real winner for all. We built enough trust in the beginning to hold it together when things got tougher at the end.

Takeaway

Lessons learned from unreasonable people in negotiating include being preemptive can discombobulate counterparties and give you advantage. Standing firm with unreasonable positions can lead to better end results. When new elements are introduced, this gives the other side license to do one plus. Though often effective, be wary of last-minute changes or unreasonable demands or tactics. These are also empowering to unreasonable teammates or clients on the other side. Internally at team meetings or client meetings, what you will hear is, "I told you we couldn't trust them." These negotiators are the ones who shift tactics and end up coming on with surprises.

CHAPTER 17

THE WINNING POWER
OF SILENCE

Speech is silver, silence is golden.

—Proverb

A Steve Jobs Strategy

A recent article in *Business Insider* titled "The Steve Jobs guide to manipulating people and getting what you want," illustrated the power of silence. The piece reported that "Jobs did not like overly complex issues, especially if they required him to make accommodations. So on occasion, he would become totally aloof. As Jobs' biographer Walter Isaacson said, 'Jobs would go silent and ignore situations that made him uncomfortable.'"[1]

Even if you haven't interacted with Steve Jobs, there is no doubt that you have experienced "the silence gap." It is most likely to occur in a conversation, during a meeting, on a sales call, or at the negotiation table. Suddenly there is a gap in the interaction. All speaking stops. Silence seems to drag on interminably. And then someone inevitably jumps in to fill the silence gap.

If you understand the power of that silence gap, you will cringe when that person jumps in. That is because whoever jumped in to fill the gap with words just lost a valuable and potentially profitable opportunity. They lost an opportunity to win a point, make a sale, or turn a negotiation from unfavorable to favorable. They failed to capitalize on the power that silence brings through discomfort.

Respect the Power of Silence

Business writer Garrett Norris describes the power of silence, saying, "Silence is an effective way to gauge the other person's confidence in their position. Many people are uncomfortable with silence and will often fill the air with meaningless talk. On the other hand, silence, when used in negotiation, always requires a response."[2] Never, ever disrespect the power of silence in a human exchange, for as many a person has observed, "Silence speaks volumes."[3]

Negotiating is about getting people to move closer to your goals. Getting people to change is a complex human process involving subtle cues and deeply personal exchanges. We all look for signals to help us navigate uncertainty and ensure the direction being taken is toward our target objective. That's why silence is so powerful, and also so discombobulating. Silence is one of the strongest and most effective tools in your negotiation skills toolbox.

Great martial artists use silence. They don't give away anything about what they are feeling or thinking. You don't know how they will move. They are silent. They are relaxed. By being silent, they can feel your intentions. They can sense what you will do next, but they can do this because their silence allows them to hear and feel you.

Silence and the Law of Supply and Demand

It's instructive to take a look at silence as a commodity through the lens of economics. The world seems to contain an over-abundance of noise and advice. Consider the fundamental law of supply and demand. The supply and demand curves tell us that as supply goes up and demand remains the same, the price goes down. This is a fundamental law of microeconomics. In today's world of massive social media communication, noise is in abundance. It's even more challenging if you live in a city. You know how noisy it can get, with constant sirens, motorcycles, trucks, traffic, construction, dogs barking, and neighbors. This abundant noise and stimulation can become overwhelming.

The need for silence is acute, and this is not just during the night for sleep. Daytime silence is important as well. So if it's noisy out there, and there's a large supply of noise, what's in short supply? Silence.

Consider these facts in support of the need for silence. People pay for meditation guidance, yoga classes, retreats, and a wide variety of trips and excursions to the woods or mountains. They are seeking quieter places where they can get away from the noise and experience peace. As the supply of noise goes up, demand for stimulation goes down, and its value drops. The demand and value of peacefulness rises, and people are willing to pay more for silence.

The Creative Component of Silence

Consider the benefits of silence through the lens of innovation. It is common that many great and imaginative thoughts, ideas, and inventions come to people during periods of silence. Creativity is enhanced by silent states such as meditation and daydreaming. This creative component of silence is also useful during negotiations and can be used as a strategy.

The "Silence Strategy" in Negotiations

The Washington Post[4] calls silence the "biggest secret to negotiations" explaining that "Silence can convey a sense of mystery and power, and it can signal one's willingness to walk away from talks rather than settle for anything less than the desired outcome." In some cases, a negotiating partner may break the silence by spilling information that strengthens the other side's hand, revealing clues about what your team is willing to accept or constraints it may be facing.

The Washington Post article goes on to point out that "Academic studies support the notion." In a white paper, law professor John Barkai of the University of Hawaii stated: "By using silence, you hope the other side will speak (to their disadvantage)." Michael Payne, a sports marketing consultant who was a marketing director for the International Olympic Committee, said silence can be particularly useful in negotiations aimed at breaking a contract—a situation that could lead to a court battle. After a prolonged silence, the opposition may yield information through which "they effectively fire themselves." They are so anxious to fill the void of silence they damage their own position so badly that you don't need to say anything else. They prove your point for you.

How to Use the "Silence Strategy" Effectively

The main principle in using the "silence strategy" effectively is to say less and listen more.

It is that simple. As your decision-makers are listening to you and pondering your strategy, when you finish, take the approach, "When you're done, you're done." Now you let them have their time. Sit back. Relax and wait. If you are having trouble staying in the silent zone, a good tactic is to imagine a peaceful place that you love. I like to think of Lake Tahoe or the old cemetery that sits on the hillside on the road to Cortona, Italy.

If you have the patience, you will see the signal that ultimately means the negotiation has turned in your favor. It will first be manifest in body language, not words. You may see the decision-makers' eyes look off into the distance; you may see them stare at your ROI and other documents. At some point, many negotiators begin to feel uncomfortable with the silence. They may feel they are not doing anything to actively move the negotiation forward. But this is not true.

Takeaway

Your silence is your most powerful negotiating strategy. Use it.

CHAPTER 18

BATTLING MIND-DRIFT

The successful warrior is the average man with laser-like focus.

—Bruce Lee

The "What did you just say?" Syndrome

You know the feeling. You have felt it. It is a sinking feeling followed by panic. Someone has been talking to you, but your mind has drifted. And now you hear the dreaded words, "So, what do you think?"

Yikes! Whether you were distracted by a Laguna Beach sunset, your own thoughts about the subject under discussion, or whether you were just plain bored and started to think about your to-do list, plans for the weekend, or what you will have for lunch, drifting happens. In meetings and negotiations, however, missing what was just said can have adverse consequences. You need to develop techniques to maintain your focus.

Mind-wandering

In their book *Psychology of Learning and Motivation*, authors Jonathan W. Schooler and James M. Broadway write, "Mind-wandering is a common everyday experience in which attention becomes disengaged from the immediate external environment and focused on internal trains of thought."[1] It's challenging to completely keep your mind focused. This is because the human mind has been designed and has evolved to be in a "ready" state. It is constantly searching for something new in its environment as a protective mechanism. It needs to be ready for whatever might happen.

In his book, *Brain-Based Learning and Education*, author Yi-Yuan Tang points out that "Mind-wandering is a common mental state involving spontaneous thought in our wakeful life such as daydreaming. Some studies show that mind-wandering occupies almost 50% of awake time... In other words, our mind is often in a divided attention state no matter what we are doing—in resting or task-related activities. This automatic operation has become the brain's default mode..."[2]

The Ready Mind

A ready mind is continuously active, and active minds tend to wander. Imagine what our ancestors would have become if they'd had a quiet mind in the middle of the Savannah. The answer is obvious: Dinner for some hungry predator. Keeping the mind ready, active, and alert is a survival mechanism for humans.

But for modern humans with different survival needs, the question of managing the ready mind remains. How should we handle our mind drift when it happens in the middle of a business meeting or important negotiation? The best approach when the counterparties notice your drift is just to tell the truth. If you "wake up" in the middle of a negotiation, the most emotionally intelligent course of action is to simply admit your drift. Stop the speaker and say, "I am so sorry, my mind drifted. Here is the last thing I remember." You may face temporary disappointment or even a rebuke for your mind-drift, depending on the relationship you have with the speaker and the importance of the conversation. But you will find that honesty about mind-drift is the best strategy in putting things right.

If you are asked what you were thinking about, be aware that you may not know it yourself. Minds don't ask for permission when they drift. So what to answer? I revert to jokingly saying I must have been thinking about my mother, when I can't remember what my mind was engaged in as it drifted away from the negotiating table.

There is always the flip side of the mind drifting issue. Suppose you are talking and the person you are speaking to gazes off into the distance or otherwise disengages. This one is easy. Just stop talking and wait. Soon the person will realize they have drifted and refocus on the conversation, probably making an apology for lack of attention. Be gracious and continue where you left off.

The Importance of Nonverbal Communication

As both a listener and a speaker, you need to pay attention to the body language of those you are engaged with during negotiation. This is especially true when speaking tone and body language diverge. Many business leaders believe that 55% of communication is body language, 38% is the tone of voice, and 7% is the actual words spoken. This is based on a study conducted in the late 1960s and later published as a book, *Nonverbal Communication*, by Albert Mehrabian.[3]

Psychology Today points out that "Albert Mehrabian is responsible for this percentage breakdown detailing the importance of nonverbal communication channels compared to verbal channels. Actually, it was two research studies (Mehrabian & Wiener, 1967 and Mehrabian & Ferris, 1967) combined that resulted in the 55/38/7 formula."[4]

The most important nonverbal clues provided through body language with respect to paying attention involve the eyes. You can train yourself to tell whether someone has drifted away from you. Just watch their eyes. An all-time great martial arts movie is *The Karate Kid* and its sequels. Mr. Miyagi, the Okinowan karate master in the movie, adopts Daniel Larusso, a bullied transfer student from New Jersey. A key part of Daniel-san's training is "focus." Mr. Miyagi says to Daniel-san, "Look eye." If their eyes look away, they are not focused, and they are not listening to you, so just stop talking. Their eyes will likely return to you once they notice your silence, and then you can resume talking. Try it.

Techniques for Managing Mind Drift

Mind drift is a real detriment to listening, focus, and successful negotiations. Here are some techniques to reduce your mind-drift tendencies.

Tactic #1—Keep your eyes on the speaker's face. If your eyes move, your mind wanders. Think about it. If you want to change your mind, you change your gaze. So keep your eyes focused, and your mind is more likely to stay focused, too.

Tactic #2—Put some distance between you and your devices. We have many modern distractions. When I was young, we didn't worry about who was trying to tweet, text, email, or call us. Nowadays, if you can see or even feel your device, it triggers a distraction. You want to see who it is. You want to check. Leave your devices where you won't be distracted by tones, sounds, or vibrations. You can check all your messages during a break. But during negotiations, keep your devices distant.

Tactic #3—Be aware of your body tension and breathe. If you come into a negotiation with tension, even if it's unrelated to the negotiation or the speaker, you will not be able to focus and be at your best. Tension draws you inward, and by definition, you are then less receptive to outside stimuli. In the Russian martial art, we use breathing and segmented tension techniques to become aware of tension and eliminate it. In basic terms, you isolate and tense various muscles while you breathe in, and relax those muscles when you breathe out. This helps raise awareness of tension and eliminate it.

Tactic #4—Embrace the tone of the speaker. Enjoy the tone and tempo of speech used by the person with whom you are engaged. This will help you focus. Everyone has a unique tone and tempo. Get in sync with it. Enjoy the differences from your own style. It will bring a fresh perspective to your negotiation.

Tactic #5—Don't "zombie-listen." While you should empty yourself of your own thoughts to focus on the words of the speaker, don't appear deadened like a zombie. Avoid being stiff, freezing up, or acting unnaturally. Become engaged with the speaker. Let your body language flow with the conversation. Nod to reinforce points you agree with, look quizzical if you don't understand, and withhold reactions or comment on points of disagreement. Even when you don't interrupt, you can influence the speaker by your body language.

Takeaway

One of the most embarrassing interpersonal situations is to be caught ignoring someone who is earnestly trying to convey something to you. The active minds of humans have strong tendencies to drift. You can reduce the likelihood of mind drift by staying physically engaged, focused, and tension-free. By engaging with the speaker through your body language, you can keep better focus on what they are saying. And if someone drifts on you, just stop talking.

A great conversation and a great negotiation are like a dance; they are rhythmic and harmonious. Remember the importance of body language and voice tone, which far outweigh the actual words spoken. If you add together the roles of body language (55%) and tone (38%) in communications, and then subtract that sum from 100%, you arrive at the shocking conclusion—the same as the Mehrabian study in the late 1960s—that only 7% of communication involves the actual words themselves.

(Note from the Mehrabian study: The above percentages were found to be most true when there was a divergence in tone and meaning.)

CHAPTER 19

ENGAGEMENT AND UNDERSTANDING

The improvement of understanding is for two ends: first, our own increase of knowledge; secondly, to enable us to deliver that knowledge to others.

—John Locke

The Three Core Aspects of Understanding

A recent article from Harvard Law School pointed out that "A relationship in negotiation is a perceived connection that can be psychological, economic, political, or personal; whatever its basis, wise leaders, like skilled negotiators, work to foster a strong connection because effective leadership truly depends on it." The article went on to suggest that, "People will view a course of action as less risky, and therefore more acceptable when it is suggested by someone that they trust."[1] The first step to building trust is understanding.

There are three aspects of understanding. The first is confirming understanding as you are engaging with a person. A second aspect of understanding is moving yourself into the other person's world; putting yourself into their shoes. A third aspect of understanding is appreciating the uniqueness of each person. These three serve to create an atmosphere of trust and build engagement during a negotiation.

Confirming Understanding

Confirming understanding is crucial to any great conversation or exchange. It is the communication by which you perceive the meaning, importance, or nature of what the other person is saying. The act of confirming understanding is by its nature an affirmation of the other person. If you say to me, "I get what you are saying," you are giving me a verbal hug. You are reinforcing me. You are telling me, "I get it."

In martial arts training, there is a lot of affirmation of understanding. In a typical training exercise, one person is the aggressor, and the other person is the receiver or defender. The aggressor will initiate an attack, and the defender or receiver will execute a technique that he has been taught. For example, the aggressor will perform a straight punch, and the receiver will execute a block and a counterpunch. The two training partners will do this over and over again. They will confirm with each other after each trial by asking, "Did I get that right?" or "How was that?" These iterations are performed repeatedly, and the confirmations are continuous. This is how martial arts techniques are "burned in."

This asking for confirmation is a valuable tool in negotiation. You can repeat or mirror back what the other person just spoke, asking if you have gotten it right. You can express being in harmony or agreement with what was said. Even when you do not agree, you can let the other person know that you have heard their statements and understand what they are saying.

Walking in the Other Person's Shoes

Another approach to understanding is what I call "perspective listening." When someone is speaking, their meaning is tied up with their perspective. The best way to think of this level of understanding is to imagine walking in the shoes of the person with whom you are speaking and communicating. Understanding at this level involves seeing the world from someone else's point of view. This can be very difficult, especially if you disagree with the person you are communicating with. However, you need to do this *especially* if you disagree with the person.

One powerful way I found to understand how another person feels is through Brazilian Jiu Jitsu, a martial art that to the common eye would look like wrestling or grappling. In Jiu Jitsu, we work from positions on our back, on the top or to the side of someone. There are techniques in this practice that cause pain which you would apply in an actual confrontation. These are called submissions. Since we don't want to hurt anyone during training, we apply pressure until they "tap out." When the pressure starts to hurt, they tap their training partner to signify "enough."

It is very important that you feel the pain or pressure that you want to inflict. You literally have to become the "victim" in order to successfully learn how to be the person applying the hold.

In understanding at this level, you hear nothing but these questions in good exchanges: "Is this right?" or "Can you feel that?" Great understanding comes from this level of exchange. You get into the other person's point of view—into their shoes.

One of the best ways to do this is to spend lots of time with your counterparty, including visiting their office, social haunts, and basically getting as much as you can into their life. Sometimes this is not possible to do physically, but sometimes it is. Even if you can't physically engage this way, through back channels and other engagements, you can learn a lot about your counterparty that can help you.

I like to think of due diligence as more than just reviewing documents and meeting management. It also includes getting to know your counterparty. To me it is like dating. When people date, they are in a variety of settings doing a variety of things. You spend enough time together in these different contexts to check your level of enjoyment from being with the other person. You spot strengths, and you spot weaknesses. You see how they react to your strengths and weaknesses. You learn their idiosyncrasies, and they learn yours. You share. You laugh. You cry. You meet their family. You meet their friends.

On a martial arts basis, watch a UFC (Ultimate Fighting Championship) or boxing match. The opponents usually "feel each other out." They pretend to kick. They pretend to punch. They feign moves to see the opponent's reaction. You see when they move forward, and you see when they retreat. During this there is very little actually fighting, at least not the kind the fans want. This early phase is the battle in a deep sense. But fans want to see contact. They are not interested in the "internal match." But if you want to be a great negotiator, you need to be obsessed with the internal match.

We were negotiating for the purchase of a company in a small town. It was a good business and had prospects if aligned with a larger company. An investment banker had marketed the company, and it was a good fit for us. We visited the company for due diligence and arranged a dinner. The prospective owner's spouse attended the dinner as well and shared how much she was looking forward to the sale and having more time with her husband, who had built a very nice company. The dinner was at a restaurant that he frequented, and we met other friends of his, all of whom congratulated him on the deal. We were at a fairly early phase of the deal, but it was clear from his wife and his friends that he was done negotiating. Without a trip to the small town, without the dinner, we would have been guessing on how much more negotiating we had to do.

Achieving this level of understanding and literally standing in or near the shoes of your counterparty will improve your negotiations and outcomes.

Getting to the "Uniqueness"

It is important to be able to distinguish a person's uniqueness from others. For this, you need to exercise your observational powers. Everyone is unique, and the more you can get to know and understand them, the better your exchanges of information and the smoother your negotiation process will be. I often have to remind people that there are roughly 7 billion people in the world, and each one has a unique set of fingerprints. It is part of your responsibility as a person who wants to exchange and engage with others to understand the other's point of view and perspective.

People tell you loudly who they are and what they care about by how they act and how they appear. Are they more external or internal? Are they dressed meticulously or casually? Are they heavily accessorized or pared down? What is their purse or wallet like? How about their shoes? Are they careful in their speech? Where are they from? There is so much you can see and hear that reveals a person—including their perspective. By answering these questions, you will be able to "walk in their shoes" and understand them much better.

Takeaway

When you confirm your understanding of the other person, listen from their perspective, and recognize their uniqueness, you build trust. Then they will find your suggestions more acceptable and be more willing to engage in productive negotiations with you. Call it human reciprocity, call it the golden rule, it is a fundamental truth that mostly you get what you give when it comes to your fellow humans.

CHAPTER 20

THE "MUST-HAVES"
OF NEGOTIATION

*In all negotiations of difficulty a man may
not look to sow and reap at once
but must prepare business and so ripen it by
degree.*

—Francis Bacon

Negotiation is an Iterative Process

Often in negotiations, participants will be judged by the result. Good negotiations lead to positive reviews and bonuses. For staff people in organizations, negotiations lead to concrete and measurable outcomes. It is a chance for an individual employee to "show their value." It is a chance for staff and teams to show their collective value to the organization in hard dollar terms.

These "8 Must-Haves" of the negotiation process will help you and your teams step inside the winners circle as successful negotiators.

#1—Awareness

Awareness in a negotiation context means understanding the entire theatre within which you are playing. The major themes around negotiation are awareness of the terrain, the parameters within which parties operate, and knowing what you and your counterparty want. Keep alert to all the variables associated with the potential transaction or resolution. If you don't get the big picture, you will miss factors that may be negotiable. Often the greatest impediment in a negotiation is not being aware of the big picture; generally, this happens when one party hasn't clearly defined what it wants. This party lacks clarity or awareness of their own goals. When one side is off, this warps the entire negotiation because the other side, by the innate structure of the situation, is responding to vague or not clearly defined goals.

The first step is to analyze and understand what you or your organization wants. The next step involves becoming aware of what the other party wants. Until you have clearly understood and are aware of what you want and what they want, negotiations cannot lead to success. If you do not know what you want, your odds of getting it go way down. If you don't know what the other side wants, you don't know what trade-offs can be made.

This most basic issue in negotiation is often overlooked or given inadequate consideration. The initial task in any negotiation is figuring out exactly what you want. This needs to be accomplished through a thorough process. Unfortunately, that exacting process often doesn't happen.

There was a supplier to one of the clients of a company of mine who was told he had to subcontract through an approved supplier. His company was not an approved supplier, although my company was. This unapproved supplier had reached out to us, and I delegated it to a VP in our organization. The VP didn't respond quickly enough, and I heard this supplier had decided to sub through another competitor of ours. I was a bit disappointed that we lost it because when I spoke with the owner, he had told me his history; he was 75 and planning retirement. This could be a nice tuck-in acquisition for us when he wanted to retire. I confronted the VP about our slow response, and he said, "We get a lot of these subcontracting inquiries, and so I didn't think it was all that different." I said, "Well, you know this guy is 75 and said he will retire soon, and we could buy this company for a nice addition to our business."

This was a failed negotiation because it didn't happen. While I wanted to blame the VP, the fact is I needed to blame myself. I didn't tell him what I was thinking in the back of my head. He didn't ask me if there was anything special, and I handed it off as if it was just another deal. The process of figuring out what you want and being aware means demanding a lot more information regarding opportunities and asking a lot more questions when given an assignment.

My advice is to become that annoying child you once met who asks you a thousand questions. If you don't use that childlike, innocent game of 1,000 questions, you run the risk of missing points that could be critical in decisions during negotiations. You will miss a vital step in identifying the full scope of what you want or need first. Always identify your needs first.

#2—Abandon Ego and Win—
Bringing Out the Best In Your Counterparty

We must take account of the human ego. A mature ego recognizes the existence of and manages the ego-centric challenges so it can focus on the issues, rise above personality clashes, and not just pursue its own determination to win. A focus on winning reduces your situational awareness. If you get what you want and the other side still declares victory, can you handle that? Can your ego handle that? The actual results are more important than the appearance of winning.

You want to bring out the best in your counterparty. Martial arts can provide great lessons in doing this. Jiu Jitsu is the gentle martial art. It looks like grappling and comes from the Samurai who brought it to Brazil, where it really developed. I have noticed during training that the more skilled the person I am training with, the better I perform. People rise to the occasion, as it were. I notice the same when I play golf. Generally, the better my golf partners, the better I play. Whatever your profession, whatever your activity, you probably notice that in your own life. Maybe it is frustrating to lose a golf game or a tennis match, but if your attitude is open and right, you learn and improve.

There are some clear reasons for this. Humans tend to mimic those we are around. I watch you move, and I can't help but mimic some of your movements. We learn so much this way. I listen to you speak, and if I am listening carefully, I will adopt some of your speech habits. In learning skills, we benefit from direct instruction given by experts. All martial arts training from the beginning of such arts is based on a teaching method of mimicking. Even how students are arranged in a martial arts class is based on this "learn by watching" approach. The teacher is in the front. The array of students is by ranking. In this manner, you are always looking forward at the teacher and those who are superior to you in training and skill.

Similarly, you don't take golf lessons from an inferior player. You take lessons from superior players certified by a respected organization. Their advanced skills are what you pay to learn from, after all. Another reason is that people will focus more and try harder in the presence of someone who is better. Appreciating their expertise brings out the best in you. At least it can if you approach it with the right attitude, one of openness, one of learning.

Apply these reasons to a negotiation, and you should want your counterparty to succeed. You should want them to be their best. I know you are thinking this is counterintuitive. We think of negotiation as having a winner and a loser. If you are representing someone else, they may want you to win. Your client does not want you to come back and say, good news, everyone got what they wanted. Sometimes your client wants the other side to fail. Sometimes they may evaluate the outcome not just on how well they did, but on how badly the other side came out in the end.

Consider the division of a pile of chips. I recall a negotiation I had with a savvy Washington, D.C., lawyer about a company I was preparing to take public. He had developed an indirect method of taking the company public, which was appealing, and we had agreed that his method would be used. However, things did not go as smoothly as initially anticipated. Not too long after we had reached that agreement, a better opportunity arose for an acquisition by a public company, and I decided to take that opportunity. This meant abandoning the lawyer's method.

The lawyer was upset and wanted compensation for the transaction that we had planned, which now was now not going to happen. He brought a claim against us, and as the documents we had signed called for mediation, we had to hire a mediator and try to settle our differences.

In approaching the mediation, I didn't think he should get much because he hadn't really done anything. He thought he should get the benefit of the bargain he would have gotten if we had completed his proposed deal.

We were a long way apart. The mediator, following usual approaches, worked to split our differences. I was frustrated to give up anything, because all we had done was sign an agreement to do something but hadn't actually taken any steps. But it was also true that I was going to benefit greatly from the new deal on the table, and the lawyer knew that. Then he said something which helped me mentally agree to a settlement. He said, "Cash, the chips on your side of the table are going to be so high, you won't be able to see mine."

Realizing the accuracy of his point, I gave him some shares in the company we were fighting about to put it behind me so I could refocus on the company. In the end, he was right. I got a lot of "chips" in the deal when we sold the company and didn't notice his.

The lawyer was a great negotiator, and I learned a lot from that negotiation. His line about the division of the pile of chips stayed with me, and I have used it many times in negotiating to get a counterparty to focus on what they are getting, not what I am getting. I appreciated his expertise and this lesson I learned, which has made me a better negotiator.

You will negotiate with egoists. You will negotiate with people obsessed with winning. You can take advantage of that. Contain your own ego and find a way for the egoist to declare victory—then you are more likely to get what you want. You can distract them with their obsession over winning.

#3—Tune into Nonverbal Signals to Help You with Backstories—Playing with Tension

Negotiators often say you should observe body language and listen to voice tones. These help you to sense feelings and ascertain what is important to the other side, pointing to opportunities where there are negotiation openings. You can, for example, pay attention to how people shake your hand—aggressive types have aggressive handshakes and will come at you hard. In contrast, shaking hands with open palms indicates a willingness to negotiate.

Negotiations are full of clues and cues. There is no question that you can become skilled at reading these nonverbal signals and using them to your advantage.

Be aware of nerves. Nerves in the negotiation context mean you are paying attention to both your tension levels and those of the other side. Tensions run high in negotiations. There is such finality to the process. There is a grade at the end. People will judge you and themselves based upon the perceived win or loss. The other side may employ various tactics designed to increase your level of tension. Please reread Chapter 12, "Say This, Not That," to remind you of word choices that increase or reduce tension. You need to know how to play with tension yourself. Breathing, as well as approaching negotiations empty and in the moment, will help reduce your level of tension and keep your mind clear and focused.

#4—Be Receptive

Being receptive in a negotiation context means that you accept that you may not get exactly what you want. You may not get exactly the terms or price that you want. However, you accept that and are willing to work through a process to discover what you can get. Receptivity is about the willingness to change.

Each party should gain from the negotiation.
—Dale Carnegie

Negotiation involves compromise. Receptiveness means you use encouraging words and body language to give the other party cues about where there is openness to compromise. It also means you leave biases behind that may hinder you from completing a transaction.

#5—Be Willing to "Play the Game"

To be engaged in a negotiation context means to be willing to "play the game" and to play it fairly. You are willing to exchange terms and engage in give and take. The give and take has to be fair also, or the deal won't happen.

Sometimes people try to skip this step, but it rarely works. A party to a negotiation may try this in a couple of ways. They might say for example, "Let's forgo the back and forth; here is our reasonable number." This will not likely be successful, as the other party will likely counter it anyway. Why? Because negotiation is always about engaging in the back and forth. The back and forth is a human need and generally accepted as part of the process. This is even true of parties who don't have to negotiate.

Another example is with best and final offers. Near the end of a negotiation a party may say, "OK, this is our best and final." But in my experience, there is always more negotiation after this. Be prepared to keep the negotiating process going, engaging with the back-and-forth discussion, until the process feels complete.

#6—Be Engaged

Engaging with a fair exchange is the heart of negotiation. Knowing that engagement is such a key part of negotiation, and that no matter what you say it is going to happen, your best bet is to think ahead about where you want to end up. Then you start imagining the back and forth that will get you there. That is what great negotiators do.

Understanding the negotiation context means you are willing to truly see things from the other party's perspective. You constantly seek to confirm that you are on the right track. This is another often overlooked, yet key element of negotiation. Like being receptive, being engaged is another key. This involves what I call "perspective listening." You listen to learn the other party's perspective. Being able to get what you want also means understanding what they want and why they want it. It means understanding the challenges facing the other side. Engagement through listening is a process that involves confirming progress and lack of progress on an ongoing basis.

Being engaged is taking the pulse of the negotiation at every stage.

#7—Use Timing and Tempo

Tempo in the negotiation context means you will use pace as a tool to get to resolution. This can start at the very beginning of the negotiation process. For face-to-face negotiations, some counterparties will use arrival times to communicate their interest in reaching agreement. If you arrive early, you are sending a message that you want to reach agreement. If your counterparty arrives late, they may be sending the message that they don't care if a deal happens or not.

During negotiations, how quickly you reply to an offer or counteroffer sends a message. Tempo in your communication sends a willingness or unwillingness to deal message. Matching someone else's speech patterns can send a signal that you would like to do something together. Speaking quickly or over someone is an aggressive move that would imply you have the upper hand.

The tempo of your actions and your communications play a role in getting deals done.

#8—Don't Give Up

Persistence in the negotiation context means you are willing to see it through. You are willing to reduce the use of games and stick to the issues for as long as it takes. Remember, breakthroughs in negotiation often happen just as people are getting "deal fatigue."

Nothing in this world can take the place of persistence. Talent will not: nothing is more common than unsuccessful men with talent. Genius will not; unrewarded genius is almost a proverb. Education will not: the world is full of educated derelicts.

Persistence and determination alone are omnipotent.
—*Calvin Coolidge*

Resolution means that you will reach agreement or recognize that no deal is going to happen. But it also means painstakingly working through each aspect and deal point. Good negotiators break down their overall objective into smaller ones. The ability to achieve a milestone in a negotiation often means gaining agreement on some basic facts.

One of the best times to get concessions is when there is "deal fatigue." Deal fatigue refers to that time where everyone is sick and tired of the negotiation. Many times, it is literally true. It happens when a dispute or a transaction has bogged down to a point where everyone is just tired of it. That is a time to suck it up and be persistent.

I remember an exercise in martial arts where we took turns doing groundwork, like in Jiu Jitsu, and just kept trading partners every few minutes, but not stopping. There were many more opportunities for submissions and many openings on both sides when we became tired. The same is true of boxers; as they get tired, they let their guard down. In negotiations, it is the same. As people tire, they get careless. If you remain persistent and alert, this gives you a great opportunity to strike a very favorable deal.

Takeaway

If you approach negotiations as an interactive, iterative process of discovery and learning, you are far more likely to get what you seek. Approaching your negotiations with an open mind, abandoning your ego, increasing your awareness, being receptive to change, and staying persistently fully engaged will lead you to success. On the other hand, if you need an ego stroke and want to simply go for the win, you are a typical negotiator. Superior negotiators find solutions that nobody saw coming and no one knew possible by engaging in the enlightened strategies in this book. I hope some of them help you.

ACKNOWLEDGEMENTS

I SPENT WELL OVER a year on this book and owe a debt of gratitude to many people, without whom this book would not exist. My approach to writing relies heavily on input from friends and professional colleagues. If an author is someone who begins at the beginning and writes until they get to the end, I am not an author. My style of writing is to collect fragments I have written, such as previous essays, combine these with my current thoughts written in snippets, shake them up, and then dump them on the floor. Then I examine them all to see what fits where and what ideas arise. I next take all that material and test it with friends and professional colleagues. I test the fragments and theories in real life situations and re-write and modify them. I also line them up against the literature I read in connection with teaching. This is anything but a linear process.

I would like to thank Dr. Marie Kaye, a book developer and editor, who had read all my books and had expressed interest in my unique perspective of blending business acumen with martial arts discipline and skills. When I decided to write a book on *Negotiation as a Martial Art*, I sent her what I had, and she helped me put many of the pieces together into what would ultimately become this book. We spoke on a near-weekly basis for three months, and not only was she a skilled editor who understood my vision, but she kept me on track, and her positive reinforcement was invaluable. Thank you, Dr. Kaye!

Both my martial arts instructors and my professors and university colleagues helped me with various concepts, probably without knowing they were doing so. Martin Wheeler, proprietor of The Academy of Beverly Hills, is one of the most thoughtful martial artists today. *Black Belt* magazine (October/November 2013) called him "The Best Kept Secret in English Speaking Martial Arts." He can relate to the similarities between physical and mental human exchanges, and we have spent many a dinner discussing these topics. Thank you, Martin, and thanks to all my other professional colleagues.

I have had the distinct pleasure of being a Professor of Practice at one of the top law schools in the country, Washington University in St. Louis. I have personally experienced the power of "learning by teaching" with some of the brightest law students in the country. The students at the law school, according to *U.S. News* (online article March 30, 2021), rank 7th in the United States among all law schools in terms of their GPAs and LSATs. They are super bright, work hard, and challenge you. They test you. Thank you to my students for making me better!

I want to give a shout out to my teammates and counterparties in 36 years of negotiations. You made me a better negotiator. I ultimately learned it is not about winning, but about discovery, learning and sharing, and tapping into the deep roots of negotiation we all carry in our DNA. Some of you pushed me into dark places, and sometimes that is where we learn the most.

Finally, thanks to the folks at Made for Success, especially my primary editor Lennie. Working with you all was like a great negotiation—a wonderful rhythmic dance. Your excellence made me better. Bravo!

ABOUT THE AUTHOR

 Cash Nickerson is chairman of AKKA North America's Business Unit. He was President, CFO, General Counsel, and the second largest shareholder of PDS Tech prior to its purchase by AKKA Technologies. Previous roles include attorney and marketing executive for Union Pacific Railroad, associate and then partner at Jenner & Block in Chicago, and chairman and CEO of an internet company. Mr. Nickerson, author of several books, is an avid writer and speaker on the workplace, jobs, and the economy. Mr. Nickerson is the founder and president of the David H. Nickerson Foundation, which supports prostate cancer research.

In addition to his leadership on the Board of Trustees, Mr. Nickerson serves on the School of Law National Council and International Council of the Whitney R. Harris World Law Institute. He is chair of both the Dallas-Fort Worth and Austin-San Antonio Regional Cabinets and chaired the North and Central Texas Regional Campaign for *Leading Together: The Campaign for Washington University.* Mr. Nickerson is the recipient of the Dallas-Fort Worth Regional Award (2009), the Global Philanthropy Award for the Harris Institute Crimes Against Humanity Initiative (2010), the School of Law Distinguished Alumni Award (2013), and the Founders Day Distinguished Alumni Award (2014). Mr. Nickerson earned his bachelor of art degree from Carleton College and his Master of Business Administration and Juris Doctor from Washington University.

Contact Information: cash@cashnickerson.com

NOTES

Author's Note

1. https://www.gse.harvard.edu/news/uk/18/01/all-educators
-are-negotiators

Introduction

1. S.C. Nickerson. *Listening As A Martial Art.* Cash Nickerson Media, Incorporated; First edition. October 12, 2015.

2. S.C. Nickerson. *The Samurai Listener.* Post Hill Press, Nashville, TN. March 6, 2018.

3. Roger Fisher and William Ury. *Getting to Yes: Negotiating Agreement Without Giving In.* Penguin Books; Updated, Revised edition. May 3, 2011.

Chapter 1: Be Like Water

1. Ken Blanchard. *Whale Done!: The Power of Positive Relationships.* Free Press, New York, NY. First edition, February 1, 2002

Chapter 2: Adjusting Your Own Position

1. Merriam-Webster. Webster's Dictionary. New Edition. Federal Street Press, Darien, CT. January 15, 2011.

2. https://www.pon.harvard.edu/daily/dealmaking-daily/negotiation -skills-and-negotiation-techniques-predicting-negotiator-decisions-and -behavior/

Chapter 3: Fixing Yourself

1. International Journal of Conflict Management ISSN: 1044-4068, September 30, 2013. https://www.emerald.com/insight/content/doi /10.1108/IJCMA-08-2012-0064/full/html

Chapter 4: Prep and Planning

1. *Forbes* magazine https://www.forbes.com/sites/robertbtucker /2019/04/08/seven-ways-to-rethink-your-next-leadership-retreat/?sh =6363c41b2650

2. FIRO B Test https://www.usgs.gov/about/organization/science -support/human-capital/firo-b-assessment

3. https://journals.sagepub.com/doi/10.1177/0018726715577707

Chapter 5: Back-to-School Mentality and Always be Training

1. https://www.gse.harvard.edu/news/uk/18/01/all-educators-are -negotiators

Chapter 7: A Mentor Is a Must

1. https://www.google.com/url?sa=t&rct=j&q=&esrc=s&source =web&cd=&ved=2ahUKEwioiqGC0ZPtAhWSmlkKHbIaDBo QFjALegQIIBAC&url=https%3A%2F%2Fwww.negotiableguide

.com%2Fpdf%2FNegotiable_Guide_for_Mentors.pdf&usg=AOvVaw3 VucEH-QU6ycP1whIcP0_0

2. https://www.inc.com/john-rampton/10-reasons-why-a-mentor-is -a-must.html

Chapter 8: The Art and Science of Memory

1. Modern Language Association https://profession.mla.org /negotiating-sites-of-memory/

2. Frontiers in Psychology–"Using Cognitive Agents to Train Negotiation Skills" https://www.ncbi.nlm.nih.gov/pmc/articles/PMC 5835330/

3. Chester Santos. *Mastering Memory: Techniques to Turn Your Brain from a Sieve to a Sponge.* Puzzlewright Press, Sterling Publishing Co., New York, NY, 2018.

Chapter 9: Listening

1. Dr. Seuss. *Green Eggs and Ham.* HarperCollins Children's Books, 2017. Originally published by Penguin Random House, LLC, 1960.

Chapter 10: Listening for Rhythm

1. William L. Ury and Bruce Patton. *Getting to Yes: Negotiating Agreement Without Giving In.* Penguin Books; Updated, Revised edition, NY, 2011.

2. Tram Nguyen & J.A. Grahn. "Mind your music: The effects of music-induced mood and arousal across different memory tasks." *Psychomusicology: Music, Mind, and Brain,* 2017, 27(2), 81-94.

Chapter 13: The Honesty Strategy

1. Hans Christian Andersen. *The Complete Fairy Tales and Stories.* Anchor (Knopf Doubleday); Anchor Folktale Literary Edition, New York, NY, 1983.

2. https://money.cnn.com/magazines/fortune/fortune_archive/1994/04/04/79125/index.htm

Chapter 16: The Value of Unreasonable People

1. https://www.inc.com/millennial-entrepreneurs/why-being-unreasonable-pays-off.html

2. Bill Shore. *The Imaginations of Unreasonable Men: Inspiration, Vision, and Purpose in the Quest to End Malaria.* Public Affairs; Reprint Edition Paperback, 2012.

Chapter 17: The Winning Power of Silence

1. https://www.businessinsider.com/steve-jobs-guide-to-getting-what-you-want-2016-10

2. https://healthybusinessbuilder.com.au/negotiation-is-silence/

3. https://dictionary.cambridge.org/dictionary/english/speak-volumes

4. https:www.washingtonpost.com/sf/brand-connect/Cadillac/wp/enterprise/this-is-the-biggest-secret-to-netotiation/

Chapter 18: Battling Mind-Drift

1. https://www.sciencedirect.com/topics/psychology/mind-wandering

2. https://www.sciencedirect.com/bookseries/psychology-of-learning-and-motivation

3. Mehrabian, A. (1972). *Nonverbal Communication.* New Brunswick: Aldine Transaction.

4. https://www.amazon.com/Brain-Based-Learning-Education-Principles-Practice

Chapter 19: Engagement and Understanding

1. https://www.pon.harvard.edu/daily/negotiation-training-daily/negotiate-relationships/

.